The Homeric Hymns

The Homeric Hymns

Susan C. Shelmerdine

Focus Publishing
R Pullins and Company
Newburyport MA

The Focus Classical Library
Series Editors • James Clauss and Albert Keith Whitaker

Hesiod's *Theogony* • Richard Caldwell • 1987
The Heracles of Euripides • Michael Halleran • 1988
Aristophanes' *Lysistrata* • Jeffrey Henderson • 1988
Sophocles' *Oedipus at Colonus* • Mary Whitlock Blundell • 1990
Euripides' *Medea* • Anthony Podlecki • 1991
Aristophanes' *Acharnians* • Jeffrey Henderson • 1992
Aristophanes' *The Clouds* • Jeffrey Henderson • 1992
The Homeric Hymns • Susan Shelmerdine • 1995
Aristophanes: *Acharnians, Lysistrata, Clouds* • Jeffrey Henderson • 1997
Euripides' *Bacchae* • Stephen Esposito • 1998
Terence: *Brothers* • Charles Mercier • 1998
Sophocles' *Antigone* • Mary Whitlock Blundell • 1998
Aristophanes' *Birds* • Jeffrey Henderson • 1999

The Focus Philosophical Library
Series Editor • Albert Keith Whitaker

Plato's *Sophist* • E. Brann, P. Kalkavage, E. Salem • 1996
Plato's *Parmenides* • Albert Keith Whitaker • 1996
Plato's *Symposium* • Avi Sharon • 1998
Plato's *Phaedo* • E. Brann, P. Kalkavage, E. Salem • 1998
Empire and the Ends of Politics • S. D. Collins and
D. Stauffer • 1999
Four Island Utopias • Diskin Clay, Andrea Purvis • 2000

ISBN 1-58510-019-6
Library of Congress 95-060147

Cover: Attic white ground covered Kylix, Apollo and a Muse (ca. 450 BC)
H. L. Pierce Fund. Courtesy, Museum of Fine Arts, Boston.

Printed in the United States of America
10 9 8 7 6 5 4 3

For my twin, Nancy

TABLE OF CONTENTS

Preface

The Homeric Hymns are a rich source of information for Greek myth, religion, language and culture. But they are more than merely scraps of ancient texts to be mined for material of interest to scholars. Long neglected in favor of the great Homeric epics to which they have been connected by name and tradition since antiquity, these poems also tell stories worth reading in their own right. The long hymns tell of a daughter stolen and her mother's grief, of one god's search for a place to found his temple, of the struggle a new-born god makes to win recognition through his skill at trickery, and of love for a mortal man imposed on a goddess to teach her a lesson. Even the shorter hymns provide wonderfully vivid portraits of the gods and goddesses in action: Zeus whispering his schemes to a trusted aunt; Athena, born from the head of her father, stopping even the sun in his course; Kastor and Polydeukes sweeping down from the heavens to save a storm-tossed ship. The hymns show in miniature many of the characteristics of the epics which have overshadowed them. Although their nature is different from that of the epics, they too deserve to find an audience.

Because the Hymns were composed by different authors and at different times, they do not all share precisely the same style and feel in the original Greek, and some have even been criticized as poor poetry. Since the aim of this translation has been to produce readable texts for a modern audience, I fear these individual traits have largely been lost in the current version. But if the Hymns sound alike in language and style here, it is worth remembering that they shared also in Greek the general language and style of early hexameter poetry. Because the Greek language operates very differently from English, using a system in which the function of a word is generally signalled by its ending, rather than by its position in the sentence, a strict literal translation is often impossible or unsatisfactory. I have tried, nevertheless, to stay as faithful as possible to the structure of each line, to translate epithets and common formulae as consistently as possible, and to allow the occasional awkwardness of the Greek to show through in the English rather than trying to correct it. Where there is a break in the text (lacuna) or lines in the manuscript that do not appear to be original, I have indicated that with dots (in the former case) and square brackets (in the latter).

I have not attempted to reproduce the rhythms or sound of the original, but I have, in most cases, used the Greek spellings of names, representing the final long ē of Greek sometimes as e and sometimes as a. In cases where the Latinized spelling has become especially well-known (e.g. Aeschylus for Aischylos, Crete for Krete), I have cheerfully abandoned ideas of consistency and used that spelling. A pronunciation guide is included to help readers not familiar with these names, and the index at the end of the book gives common Latin spellings and names in brackets after their Greek equivalents.

The notes have been written with two audiences in mind: the novice reader of early Greek poetry and the more experienced reader of classical literature. For the former I have tried to identify important characters, places and concepts mentioned in the text, for the latter I have added background information and more speculative commentary. The discussion of themes within the narratives will, I hope, be of interest to both and will provide an incentive to explore other themes not mentioned here. My advice to the novice reader is to read each hymn first without the notes, except where clarification is needed, so the narrative will not be too often interrupted with secondary information before it can be appreciated on its own.

The General Introduction offers information about the collection (corpus) of the hymns and treats four main topics, the literary tradition of Greek poetry and its varying subject matter, sources for the study of Greek myth, the form and nature of the hymns, and the performance of the hymns. A chronological table of major Greek authors is provided for context, and a genealogical chart of the gods (based largely on Hesiod's *Theogony*) is included for reference. Two maps are also included for those not familiar with Greece and its environs. The illustrations from ancient sculpture and vase-painting are reproduced both for fun and to remind us that what we know about the gods and their myths comes from the plastic arts as well as from literature. Each hymn is preceded by its own introductory note on the date and place of the hymn's composition (usually unknown, alas) and on other main points of interest. A list of suggestions for further reading precedes the pronunciation guide and index at the end of the book.

The translation is based on the Oxford text edited by T.W. Allen, supplemented by the commentaries listed in the suggested readings. In addition to these, I have benefited especially from the editions of

M.L. West on the *Theogony* (Oxford 1966) and the *Works and Days* (Oxford 1978), and from the Cambridge commentaries on the Iliad (vol. 1-6) and the Oxford commentaries on the *Odyssey* (vol. 1-3).

I am grateful to my colleagues in Greensboro and elsewhere who read or used early drafts of this translation in their classes and to Jeffrey Patton who patiently drew and redrew the maps to show as many locations in the hymns as possible. I offer special thanks to Theresa Rotante, David Wharton, and Sarah Wright, all of whom endured several early versions of the text and improved both translation and notes with their tactful comments. My thanks go also to James J. Clauss and Michael R. Halleran for their helpful criticisms and suggestions on the final manuscript. I dedicate this book to the memory of my twin sister, Nancy.

S.C. Shelmerdine
University of North Carolina at Greensboro

The following abbreviations appear in the introduction and notes:

A.	Aeschylus
Ant. Lib.	Antoninus Liberalis
Apollodorus	Apollodorus, *Library*
E.	Euripides
h. *Ap.*	Homeric *Hymn to Apollo*
h. *Aph.*	Homeric *Hymn to Aphrodite*
h. *Dem.*	Homeric *Hymn to Demeter*
h. *Dion.*	Homeric *Hymn to Dionysos*
h. *H.*	Homeric *Hymn to Hermes*
h. 1, h. 6-34	shorter Homeric Hymns to different deities
Il.	Homer, *Iliad*
Met.	Ovid, *Metamorphoses*
Od.	Homer, *Odyssey*
Paus.	Pausanias, *Description of Greece*
Pi.	Pindar, Odes: *Olympian* (O.), *Pythian* (P.), *Nemean* (N.)
Pliny, *NH*	Pliny, *Natural Histories*
S.	Sophocles
Th.	Hesiod, *Theogony*
WD	Hesiod, *Works and Days*

Illustrations

General Introduction

The Homeric Hymns are a collection of thirty-three poems written in dactylic hexameter, like the *Iliad* and *Odyssey*, but composed by different authors over a span of many centuries, from the 8th-century BC to as late as the Hellenistic period. The Hymns fall into two groups: four major poems (to Demeter, Apollo, Hermes and Aphrodite) ranging in length from 293 to 580 lines, and twenty-nine minor poems of 3 to 59 lines. Each of the longer poems tells a story about the god or goddess to whom it is addressed, while the shorter hymns are often only invocations.

Collected in antiquity, the Hymns survive today in thirty-one different manuscripts: 29 late Byzantine manuscripts and 3 fragments of papyrus. How they came to be collected is uncertain, but some manuscripts preserved them along with the Homeric poems, while others grouped them with selections from such authors as Hesiod, Pindar, Orpheus, Proclus, and Callimachus. With the exception of one 15th-century manuscript (M), which preserves the opening of the first *Hymn to Dionysos* and the entire *Hymn to Demeter*, all others begin with the *Hymn to Apollo*.

The Literary Tradition and Its Subject Matter. Although the Hymns were composed at very different times, they all belong to a tradition identified with Homer. A word about this tradition, therefore, and about the stages of Greek literature which immediately followed it may be in order. The earliest surviving works of Greek literature come from the body of hexameter poetry associated with Homer and Hesiod (see chronological table). The individual poems were developed over many generations, as different singers composed and retold favorite stories, and an oral tradition grew up. As a result, it is not possible to say for certain who composed, sang, or even dictated the poems which have survived. If a poet named Homer actually existed, it is not clear what role he played in the development of the poems attributed to him, so modern scholars often speak instead of the tradition in which he, and other poets, worked. The Homeric tradition, which may have originated in Ionia (Map 1), is characterized by the heroic poetry of the *Iliad* and *Odyssey*, poems which tell of Achilles' anger in the war against Troy, and of the return to Greece of resourceful Odysseus after the same war. The Hesiodic tradition, which began on the mainland of Greece in Boiotia (Map 1), preserves didactic and catalogue poetry such as the *Works and Days* (a poem of advice on how mankind should live in an often harsh world), the *Theogony* (an account of how the Greek gods came into existence and consolidated their power in the universe), and the *Catalogue of Women* (a series of short biographies detailing the divine loves and famous offspring of women). Because the origins of this poetry lie in an oral tradition, it is impossible to say with certainty which poem came first, or even, very often, which tradition influenced the other. The Homeric and Hesiodic poems which survive were probably composed in the 8th-century BC. (see Table 1), but not preserved in a fixed, written text until as late as the 6th-century BC when contests involving recitations of heroic poetry became a part of certain festivals in the Greek world.

Also connected with the body of early hexameter poetry are the poems of the so-called Epic Cycle which told a variety of heroic legends from the beginning of the world through the death of Odysseus.

Table 1

Poem	Major Event
Titanomachy	Theogony and Battle of Titans
"Theban Cycle"	
Oedipodeia	Story of Oedipus
Thebais	Quarrel between Eteocles and Polyneices
Epigoni	Sack of Thebes
"Trojan Cycle"	
Cypria (11 books)	Causes and First nine years of Trojan War
Iliad (24 books)	Anger of Achilles
Aethiopis (5 books)	Death of Achilles and Dispute over his armor
Little Iliad (4 books)	Trojan Horse and Fall of Troy
Iliou Persis (2 books)	Madness of Aias, Arrival of Philoctetes, Sack of Troy
Nostoi (5 books)	Return home of Agamemnon, Menelaos, and other Greek heroes
Odyssey (24 books)	Odysseus' return home
Teleony (2 books)	Death of Odysseus and its aftermath

Like the Hymns, these poems were composed at widely different times and by different authors, but unlike the Hymns, their subject matter concentrates on the heroes of early Greek legend. In general, these poems are considered to be later than the Homeric and Hesiodic works, dating perhaps to the 6th- and 5th-centuries BC. This judgment is made both on grounds of diction and because the poems of the Cycle seem to concentrate on myths not already contained in the works of Homer and Hesiod. Although the poems of the Cycle do not survive except in fragments and in the summaries of later authors, we are able to identify the title and content of many. Table 1 arranges the heroic poems in the chronological order of the myths they tell.

The poems of the Cycle, as well as other stories about the life of "Homer", were sung by a guild of singers known as the Homeridai ("Sons of Homer") who were active on the island of Chios (Map 1) at least by the end of the 6th-century BC. These Homeridai and other rhapsodies like them recited traditional songs in contests at festivals like the Panathenaia in Athens. The 7th- and 6th-centuries BC ushered in the Archaic Age which saw the rise and flowering of lyric poetry, so-called because the poems were sung to the accompaniment of a musical instrument, usually the lyre. These poems were generally short pieces composed in a variety of meters for performance either by an individual ("monody") or a chorus ("choral lyric"). Poetry sung to the flute ("elegy") also flourished at this time. Unlike the largely anonymous poets of earlier hexameter tradition, the major poets of this period can be identified and often linked with specific islands or cities, and the poems themselves show distinct regional dialects. Archilochus, for example, was born on the island of Paros; Semonides flourished on Samos, Sappho and Alcaeus on Lesbos, and Alcman and Tyrtaeus in Sparta (see Map 1). The poetry of these authors was also characterized by a much more personal outlook and tone than that of the earlier hexameter poems. Archilochus and Semonides both wrote iambic poetry (so-called from its meter) of a satiric and insulting tone, the former rejecting the traditional heroic view of war, love, and society in general, the latter attacking women. Callinus (in Ionia) and Tyrtaeus composed elegiac poetry on heroic and martial themes, and Theognis used the same meter to comment on the political and social climate of his day. Alcman and, later, Simonides wrote choral lyrics for a variety of specific occasions, producing maiden songs, wedding songs, dirges, epigrams and other works. The poems of Sappho and Alcaeus are more personal, celebrating the pleasures of love and wine, and sometimes commenting on local politics. For this reason, most lyric poetry of the archaic period provides less material for the study of Greek myth than early hexameter. Notable exceptions include the hymns of Alcaeus and the choral lyrics of Stesichoros and Ibycos, who both wrote narrative poems on the adventures of Herakles and other heroes of the epic cycle. By the 6th century, the first works of prose were also being written, in the form of early philosophical treatises, of which only fragments remain.

Lyric poetry continued to thrive at the beginning of the 5th-century BC, especially in the choral lyrics of Pindar in Thebes and Bacchylides on Kos (Map 1). The victory odes of Pindar and his contemporaries, composed for athletes at the Olympic and other games, took up again the telling of traditional myths and connected them to personal and historical events of their own day. Although the connection between the myth and the occasion being celebrated is not always clear, these poems provide a rich store of mythic material for study. The poetry of Bacchylides, by including passages of dialogue within the narrative (and sometimes in their own right), marks a transition from lyric poetry to tragedy. In the last half of this century, the great tragedians, Aeschylus, Sophocles and Euripides, reworked traditional stories for the stage and tragedies became an important part of annual festivals in many cities. At the same time, Aristophanes and others began to produce comedies, and prose writers such as the historians Herodotus and Thucydides began to come into prominence.

During the 4th-century BC, writers of comedy (Menander), history (Xenophon), philosophy (Plato, Aristotle), and oratory (Lysias, Demosthenes) expanded the diverse corpus of Greek literature, but the 3rd century saw a return, at least by some authors, to the genres and subject matter of the earlier periods. Among the most important of these, the poet Callimachus wrote short pieces, including hymns, and Apollonius Rhodius turned again to hexameter epic for the story of Jason and the Argonauts.

Sources for Greek Myth. The preceding survey of Greek literary traditions has indicated several sources for the study of Greek myth, primarily in the poetry of each century. But the ancients also had a great interest in collecting and commenting on the traditional myths. With the exception of works in the Hesiodic tradition, most of these mythological collections are relatively late and many are now lost to us. Among the best known in modern times is the *Bibliotheca* of Apollodorus, a summary of Greek myths and legends written perhaps in the 1st- or 2nd-century AD. Only three books of the whole work survive, but they are valuable for recording different versions of many myths and for their citations of Apollodorus' sources, many of which are now lost. Eratosthenes (c. 275-194 BC), who became head of the Alexandrian Library, wrote a treatise on constellations and their mythology (through metamorphosis), and a short epic on the birth and rise of Hermes. These works are now lost, but a later epitome of the treatise on constellations does survive. Antoninus Liberalis (2nd-c. AD?) wrote a collection of metamorphoses, and Hyginus (2nd-c. AD?) wrote, in Latin, a handbook of mythology called the *Fabulae* based on Greek sources. Of this last work only a series of late and unreliable extracts survives.

Another source for Greek mythology is the representations of gods, heroes and sometimes the myths themselves in Greek art. Gods can often be recognized by their attributes: Zeus with his thunderbolt (fig. 4), Poseidon with a trident and/or fish (fig. 3), Athena often helmeted, with spear and a shield or aegis (figs. 4, 5, 6), Apollo with a lyre (cover), Artemis with bow, quiver and, often, an animal (fig. 2), and Hermes with winged sandals, traveler's cap and a staff or cadeuceus (figs. 1, 4, 6). On some vases, names are even inscribed to identify different figures (fig. 1). By contrast, Hera and Aphrodite frequently appear without attributes and can be difficult to identify without other clues (fig. 6).

Representations of the myths told in the Homeric Hymns also exist, although not in abundance. A red figure krater (a bowl for mixing wine) from the mid-5th-century BC shows Persephone (labeled "Persephata" on the vase) rising from the Underworld as Hermes stands near, while Hekate, holding two torches and looking back at the maiden, moves toward Demeter at the right (fig. 1). A black figure hydria (water jar) from the last decades of the 6th-century BC shows two scenes from the story of Hermes' theft of Apollo's cattle (fig. 7a-c). On one side of the vase, five of the cattle stand in a cave (represented on the vase by a curving bush, fig. 7b), while on the other, the baby Hermes lies in his bed (which looks rather like a t.v. stand) as three standing figures (Apollo, Maia and another unidentified male) appear to argue over him (fig. 7c). That the details of these scenes do not exactly match the stories told in the extant hymns is not surprising, given the long oral tradition which lies behind the texts we have. If Persephone was called Persephata in some versions of the Demeter myth, or Maia had a husband or male servants in another version of the Hermes story, there is no reason these variants shouldn't appear on vases as well as in written accounts.

By the same token, it is not possible to connect a given artistic representation to a specific text with any certainty. While a winged Eos appears with her lover, Tithonos, on the inside of a red figure kylix (cup) from the early part of the 5th-century BC (fig.9), there is no evidence to suggest that the specific text of the *Hymn to Aphrodite* was in the painter's mind. The same is true for the scene inside a black figure kylix from the mid-6th-century (fig. 11): Dionysos, holding his characteristic drinking cup, reclines in a ship as the mast is entwined with grape vines and dolphins swim on all sides. Even so, while there is no reason to suppose the painter knew the hymn rather than some other account of the story, it is tempting to see in this picture the scene described in the *Hymn to Dionysos* (35ff.).

The Form and Nature of the Hymns. The Homeric Hymns are so called because their style, language, and meter are so similar to that of the Homeric epics. The word *humnos* in Greek originally described a song celebrating a god or goddess and, at least in its early uses, did not have the same connotations as our word "hymn". Its only use in Homer refers generically to the song sung after a meal, and other early uses are similarly vague. While the hymns were composed at widely different times, their form is quite regular and is well-illustrated by the *Hymn to Hermes*:

> *Introduction.*
> <u>Sing, Muse,</u> of <u>Hermes, son of Zeus and Maia,</u>
> ruler of <u>Kyllene</u> and Arcadia rich in flocks,
> <u>swift messenger of the immortals,</u> <u>whom</u> Maia bore,
> the reverent nymph with the beautiful hair, mingling
>   in love with Zeus.

The poet begins by naming his subject ("Hermes") and sometimes, as here, calling on the gods for inspiration ("Sing, Muse"). The naming of the god is often accompanied, as it is here, by mention of his parents ("son of Zeus and Maia"), and/or his place of birth ("Kyllene"). One or more epithets defining the domain of the god complete his identification ("swift messenger of the immortals"), before the poet begins to celebrate those powers in the body of the song, usually introduced by a relative pronoun ("whom...").

Middle. The middle section of the hymn allows more variation than either the beginning or the end and occurs in all the hymns except h. 13 (to Demeter). In the *Hymn to Hermes*, as in about a dozen others, the introduction is followed immediately by a myth or narrative portion which describes past events in the life of the deity. In some of the hymns, the mythic section is preceded, or even replaced, by a section which describes the attributes of the god, usually in the present tense. Hymns 11 (to Athena) and 12 (to Hera) provide good examples of hymns without a myth, while h. *Ap.* 2-14 illustrates the use of this "attributive" section before the myth itself.

Closing. The end of the hymn is as regular as its opening. In the *Hymn to Hermes* the singer bids farewell to his subject, but promises to remember him as he moves on to a new song: "And so farewell, son of Zeus and Maia / and I will remember you and another song too." The farewell to the deity occurs in all hymns except h. *Dem.* and h. 24, while the reference to moving on to another song occurs in three of the four long hymns and about half of the shorter ones. Another element sometimes found at the conclusion of the hymn is a prayer to the deity (e.g. h. 6 "grant that I may carry off the victory in the contest, and inspire my song").

The five-line hymn to the twins Kastor and Polydeukes (h. 17) preserves a good outline of the hymnic form, with most of the elements mentioned above: Introduction (1-2), Myth (3-4), Closing (5):

> Sing, clear-voiced Muse, of Kastor and Polydeukes
> the Tyndaridai who were born from Olympian Zeus.
> Beneath the peak of Taygetos queenly Leda bore them
> having yielded in secret to the dark-clouded son of Kronos.
> Farewell, Tyndaridai, riders of swift horses.

The nature of the hymns is less easy to specify, since we know so little about their authors or the context in which they were created. Pausanias quotes from five writers of hymns, Olen, Pamphos, Homer, Musaeus and Orpheus. Of these, all but Homer can be linked with specific places of worship. Olen, for example, was said to have come from Lycia (in south-west Asia Minor) to Delos and to have written hymns for the worship of the deities there (Paus. 1.18.5, Hdt. 4.35). Pamphos and Orpheus are linked with choral hymns written for the Athenians, and Musaeus with hymns for performance in the rites at Eleusis. However mythical the hymnists themselves remain, the poems attributed to these four poets differ from those attributed to Homer, both in their local character and in their choral performance. By contrast, the Homeric Hymns seem to have been composed for recitation by one singer and appear more literary than devotional in nature. Rather than being clearly connected to the worship of local deities, these hymns seem intended as companion pieces to other epic narratives.

Thucydides (3.104) quotes a few lines from the *Hymn to Apollo*, calling it a *prooimion* or "prelude," and Pindar seems to link the performance of epic poetry to just such *prooimia* (*N.* 2.1-5):

> Just as the Homeridai,
> singers of woven stories, often
> begin with a prelude to Zeus, ...

This evidence is supported by the final lines of two Homeric Hymns which refer specifically to the poet singing the deeds of men (epic poetry) after beginning with a hymn to the god (h. 31.18-19, h. 32.18-20), and the typical hymnic ending formula which contains a promise by the poet to sing another song. Hymns 1 and 7 add a tribute to the importance of the god (in both cases, Dionysos) for inspiring the poet (h. 1.17-18 "we singers hymn you as we begin and end, and there is no way/for the poet who forgets you to remember his sacred song"). Even if the later hymns preserved these formulaic endings merely as literary devices, it seems reasonable to conclude that the hymns were originally intended as preludes to the recitations of other songs, including epic narratives. Indeed the long poems of Hesiod preserve preludes in their opening lines (*WD* 1-10 to Zeus; *Th*. 1-115 to the Muses), and Crates of Mallos, the first librarian at Pergamum, evidently knew a version of the *Iliad* which began with a hymn ("I sing of the Muses and Apollo famous for his bow").

The Performance of the Hymns. If the hymns were originally composed as preludes to longer songs, this function also appears to have evolved over time into something different. The longer hymns as we have them, for instance, are probably too long to have been preludes and may have served as the main event of a given performance. Similarly, although the *Odyssey* presents the performance of epic poetry as informal entertainment at the end of the evening meal, the extant versions of the *Iliad* and *Odyssey* are each too long to have been performed in one evening. We know, however, that at least by the 6th-century BC Homer's poems came to be performed in the formal context of contests at sacred festivals such as the Panathenaia in Athens. The hymns too may well have been performed at both informal and formal occasions. Given this assumption, the evidence of the ancient poems must be treated cautiously.

It is clear that not only Homer's epics, but other hexameter poetry, including hymns, were performed in contests. Hymn 6.19-20 explicitly asks the goddess Aphrodite to grant the poet "victory in the contest," but gives no other details of its performance. Hesiod (*WD* 654-659) speaks of winning a tripod, which he dedicated to the Muses of Helikon at the funeral games of a man named Amphidamos. And a three line fragment from the Hesiodic corpus refers to a poetic contest between Homer and Hesiod which seems to have occurred at the Delian festival in honor of Apollo (fr. 256):

> On Delos then did Homer and I first as singers,
> stitching a theme in new hymns, celebrate with song and dance
> Phoibos Apollo with the golden sword, whom Leto bore…

This festival, or one like it, is described in the *Hymn to Apollo* (see note on lines 146-164), where the poet mentions a series of different songs performed by the chorus of Delian maidens (158-161): first a hymn to Apollo, then to Leto and Artemis, and finally a heroic narrative "remembering men and women of old." This description supports the view of the hymns as preludes to epic poetry. Hymn 26.12-13 also seems to refer to an annual festival, this one in honor of Dionysos as it closes with the wish that the poet and others may "come rejoicing again next year."

In addition to their performance as preludes to heroic narratives and as a part of contests both in religious festivals and at funeral games, the hymns may also have been performed in less formal settings. In the *Hymn to Hermes* (54-56), Hermes' first song, itself a hymn, recalls to the poet the songs of young men at feasts, and his second song, a theogony, is also compared by Apollo to the deeds of young men at a feast (453-454). Neither passage makes clear whether the feasts occur in the context of a festival or other ritual event, but evidence from the Homeric epics attests to the central place of poetic performances at private banquets. At the palace of Odysseus the singer, Phemios, entertains the suitors at the end of the meal as he sings epic songs to the accompaniment of his lyre (*Od.* 1.152-155, 325-327). At the court of the Phaiakians, Demodokos provides similar entertainment (*Od.* 8.72-82, 485-520).

In Phaiakia we also see another context for the performance of songs, when Demodokos sings in the midst of a circle of dancers, telling the light-hearted story of the love of Ares and Aphrodite (*Od.* 8.256-366). In this scene, it is not clear whether the dancers re-enact the events of the story or simply dance in response to the music itself, but the scene is one of several which show the combination of song and dance in Homer's world (cf. *Il.* 18.491-495, 567-572, 590-605; *Od.* 1.152, 23.133-147). According to the testimony of the hymns, the Homeric scenes are paralleled on Olympos as well. In the *Hymn to Hermes*, Apollo declares himself a follower of "the Olympian Muses who care for dances and the glorious paths of song and rich music" (450-452) and, in the *Hymn to Apollo*, the same god goes to Olympos with his lyre and stirs at once an interest in song and dance among the immortals. As he plays, the Muses sing songs about gods and men, while the other gods and goddesses dance (h. *Ap.* 182-206).

From these sources, then, it is clear that song, dance, and lyre-playing were found in various combinations and in many different settings. That preludes such as the Homeric Hymns found a place in the full variety of these settings seems likely. The shorter hymns could easily have functioned as true preludes to the performance of other songs, while the longer hymns may have been performed by themselves as set pieces in contests or as pure entertainment in more in formal contexts. It is easy to imagine the hymns to Demeter or Apollo sung in the context of religious festivals in honor of those gods, but it is equally easy to picture the hymns to Hermes or Aphrodite performed in a context similar to that in which Demodokos sang the story of Ares and Aphrodite. In either case, the possibility exists that these performances contained dance as well as song.

CHRONOLOGICAL TABLE

The dates of many authors and works listed below are quite uncertain and are offered here only as rough guidelines.

Date	Author/Work	Genre
8TH-CENTURY BC		
750	Homer, *Iliad*	epic
	Homer, *Odyssey*	epic
7TH-CENTURY BC		
	Hesiod, *Theogony*	genealogical poetry
ca. 690	*Hymn to Apollo* (Delian)	hymn
ca. 675	*Hymn to Aphrodite*	hymn
	Hesiod, *Works and Days*	didactic poetry
	Archilochus	elegy and iambic poetry
ca. 675-625	*Hymn to Demeter*	hymn
650	Callinus	elegy
	Semonides	iambic poetry
	Tyrtaeus	elegy
	Alcman	choral lyric
	Stesichoros	choral lyric
	Sappho	lyric poetry
	Alcaeus	lyric poetry
6TH-CENTURY BC		
ca. 585	*Hymn to Apollo* (Pythian)	hymn
	Ibykos	lyric poetry
550	Theognis	elegy
	Simonides (557-468)	choral lyric
	Anacreon	lyric poetry
	Aeschylus (525-456)	tragedy
ca. 510	*Hymn to Hermes*	hymn
	Pindar (522-438?)	choral lyric
5TH-CENTURY BC		
	Bacchylides (510-450)	choral lyric
	Sophocles (c.496-406)	tragedy
	Euripides (485-406)	tragedy
	Herodotus (c. 484-425)	history
	Thucydides (c. 460-400)	history
	Aristophanes (c. 445-380)	comedy
4TH-CENTURY BC		
	Lysias (c. 459-380)	oratory
	Xenophon (c. 428-355)	history
	Plato (427-347)	philosophy
	Demosthenes (384-322)	oratory
	Aristotle (384-322)	philosophy
	Menander (c. 342-293)	comedy

Genealogy of the Gods
Primary Source: Hesiod, *Theogony*

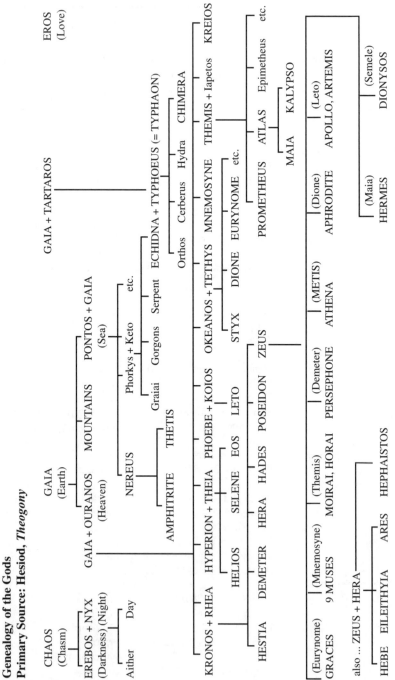

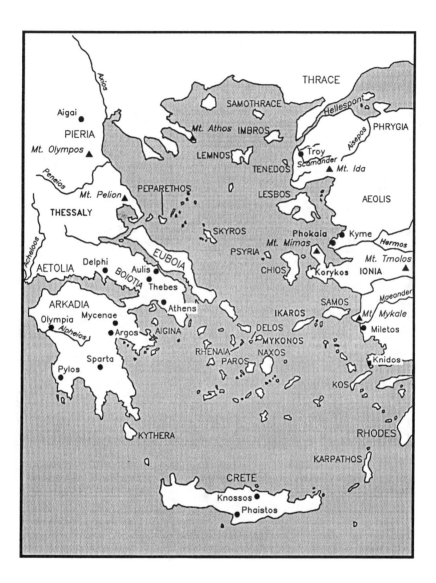

Map 1 Greece and the Aegean Islands

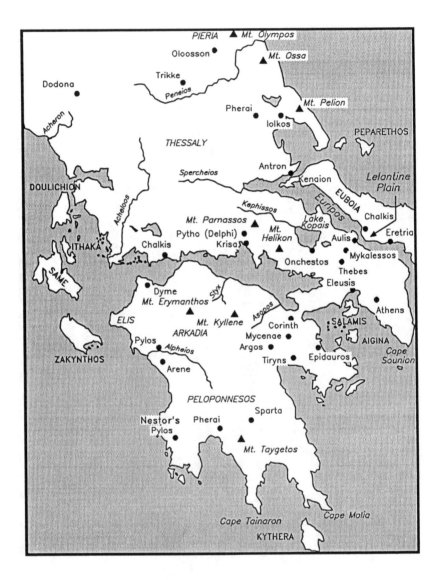

Map 2 Mainland Greece

Vase Paintings with Mythological Themes

1. Return of Persephone

Courtesy, The Metropolitan Museum of Art,
Fletcher Fund, 1928. (28.57.23)

2. Artemis
James Fund and by Special Contribution
Courtesy, Museum of Fine Arts, Boston

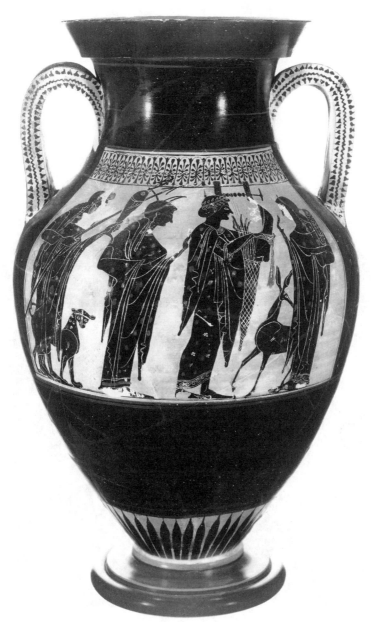

3. Poseidon with Leto
John Michael Rodocanachi Fund
Courtesy, Museum of Fine Arts, Boston

4. Birth of Athena
H. L. Pierce Fund
Courtesy, Museum of Fine Arts, Boston

5. Athena wearing the aegis
Gift of Samuel Dennis Warren and Everett Fund
Courtesy, Museum of Fine Arts, Boston

6. Hera, Athena, Aphrodite, and Hermes
Seth Kettell Sweetser Fund
Courtesy, Museum of Fine Arts, Boston

7a. Infant Hermes with stolen cattle
Courtesy, Musée du Louvre, Départment des Antiquités Grecques,
étrusques et romaines. Photographie M. Chuzeville

7b. Stolen Cattle
Courtesy, Musée du Louvre, Départment des Antiquités Grecques,
étrusques et romaines. Photographie M. Chuzeville

7c. Infant Hermes
Courtesy, Musée du Louvre, Départment des Antiquités Grecques,
étrusques et romaines. Photographie M. Chuzeville

8. Apollo and Muse
H. L. Pierce Fund
Courtesy, Muesum of Fine Arts, Boston

9. Eos and Tithonos
Catharine Page Perkins Collection
Courtesy, Muesum of Fine Arts, Boston

10. Dionysos with a Satyr and a Maenad
Courtesy, Arthur M. Sackler Museum, Cambridge

11. Dionysos in ship
Courtesy, Antikensammlungen, Munich

1. HYMN TO DIONYSOS°

For some say it was at Drakanon,° others on wind-swept Ikaros,
and some say on Naxos, heaven-born Eiraphiotes,°
but others by the deep-eddying river Alpheios
that Semele° conceived and bore you to Zeus who delights in thunder.

HYMN TO DIONYSOS   The first 9 lines of this hymn are quoted by
Diodorus Siculus (3.66.3), who attributes them to Homer himself, while
lines 10-21 are preserved in the same manuscript (M) which contains the
hymn to Demeter and the other long Homeric hymns. There is no
absolute proof that the two sections belong to the same poem, but there is
equally no reason to suspect they do not. Both the placement of the hymn
at the beginning of the manuscript preceding those to Demeter, Apollo,
Hermes, and Aphrodite, and the formulaic final lines suggest that this
hymn was originally of a length similar to the other long hymns in the
corpus. We have no real evidence for its date or place of composition. Like
the *Hymn to Apollo*, the *Hymn to Dionysos* seems to deal first with the birth
of the god, and then with the origins of his festival.

1   The poet begins with a catalogue of possible birth-places for the god.
Drakanon was a cape on the island of Kos, Ikaros an island near Samos,
and Naxos one of the Cyclades islands (see Map 1). The Alpheios river
was on the mainland of Greece in Elis (see Map 2). All these sites
boasted connections with the worship of Dionysos in antiquity.

2   The meaning of Dionysos' epithet *eiraphiotes* is obscure. Among the
many ancient explanations given is its connection to the Greek word for
"sew" (*rhaptô*) and thus its potential allusion to the myth of Dionysos'
birth from Semele (see below).

4   Semele was one of the daughters of Kadmos, a legendary ruler of
Thebes in Boiotia, and his wife Harmonia, herself the daughter of Ares
and Aphrodite. According to myth, Zeus conducted an affair with
Semele which ended when she, already pregnant, asked Zeus to appear
to her as he would to his wife, Hera. Bound by an unbreakable oath to
grant her wish, Zeus appeared in his full glory and the mortal Semele
was at once consumed by his fiery essence. Zeus snatched the unborn
Dionysos from her womb as she was engulfed by the flames and placed
(or "sewed") the premature god in his own thigh, from which he gave
birth to Dionysos later. From this story comes Dionysos' common
epithet "twice-born."

And others, lord, say that you were born in Thebes   5
but they are lying, for the father of men and gods bore you
far away from men, hiding you from whitearmed Hera.

There is a certain Nysa,° a very high mountain blooming with
    forests
far from Phoinike, near the streams of Aigyptos°
. . . .
and for her they will set up many offerings in her temples.   10
As he cut you into three pieces,° so always in biennial festivals
will men sacrifice complete hecatombs to you."

The son of Kronos° spoke and nodded with his dark brows,
and the ambrosial hair of the lord flowed down
from his immortal head, and he caused great Olympos to shake.   15
So having spoken Zeus the deviser gave orders with a nod of his
    head.

Be propitious, Eiraphiotes, you who drive women mad.° We singers
hymn you as we begin and end, and there is no way
for the poet who forgets you to remember his sacred song.

And so farewell to you, Dionysos Eiraphiotes,   20
with your mother Semele, whom they call Thyone.°

---

8   Nysa was a common place-name in antiquity (see h. *Dem.* 17n.), but here evidently refers to a site somewhere in Egypt. A popular etymology for the god's name derives "Dionysos" from the word *Dios* (another form of Zeus' name) and *Nysa*, the god's birthplace.

9   Diodorus' quotation ends here and if this portion of the hymn belongs with lines 10-21 there is a break of indeterminate length in the text at this point. The "her" of the next line appears to be Semele, Dionysos' mother.

11   The reading of the manuscript for this line is garbled beyond hope and the translation here accepts an emended version of the text. There was a version of Dionysos' myth in which he was torn to pieces by the Titans, but if this is alluded to here the singular "he" is odd.

13   "The son of Kronos" is a common epithet for Zeus

17   Dionysos was said to drive women mad because of the ecstatic frenzy which took hold of them during their worship of him, cf. Euripides' *Bacchae.*

21   In different ancient sources Thyone is alternately the name of Dionysos' mother, his nurse, or a maenad.

2. HYMN TO DEMETER

Introduction

The *Hymn to Demeter* was probably composed around 675-625 BC and provides the earliest literary evidence for the cult of Demeter at Eleusis, a town roughly fourteen miles west of Athens (see Map 2). How closely it reflects the actual practice of those rites is a matter of debate among scholars, but many details in the narrative can be tied directly to what we know of the celebrations at Eleusis. One new theory (Clinton, K. *Myth and Cult: The Iconography of the Eleusinian Mysteries* [Stockholm 1992]) suggests that the hymn provides an aetiological myth for the Thesmophoria, a women's festival in honor of Demeter, but that case seems less persuasive. Nothing is known about the poet who composed this hymn.

It has been argued that the hymn deals with two separate myths which it never fully connects: (1) Persephone's abduction and (2) the institution of the Eleusinian Mysteries. The first myth belongs to a group of traditional stories about young women (and boys) stolen away by amorous men who must eventually settle their claims with the victim's parents (or family). In this category are the myths of Zeus and Europa, Zeus and Ganymede, Poseidon and Pelops, and even Paris and Helen. The theme of abduction in these stories, however, is often woven together with other themes such as, in the Paris and Helen myth, the themes of "the journey," "the sacking of a city" and "the withdrawal of the hero." In the *Iliad* it is the last thread which predominates, as the poem focuses on Achilles' withdrawal from battle rather than on the abduction of Helen. Since Persephone is often associated with the new bloom of plants in spring, the story of her abduction by Hades has also been said to contain elements common to the theme of the "marriage of a fertility goddess." But the hymn as we have it subordinates this theme to the story of Demeter's withdrawal and journey to Eleusis after her daughter's disappearance. This is the part of the hymn which appears most closely tied to the institution of the cult at Eleusis.

Very little is known for certain about the Eleusinian cult which was the most famous of many so called mystery religions in the ancient world. Clement of Alexandria, a Christian writer born around 150 AD, records the password of the initiates, "I fasted, I drank from the *kykeon*, took out of the *kistê* [a round box tied with purple ribbons], worked, placed back in the basket and from the basket into the *kistê*," but provides no details. The outline of the rite which follows, then, is guesswork based largely on late accounts.

The full ritual included the Lesser Mysteries, which took place in Athens seven months before the rite at Eleusis and which involved some kind of preliminary purification. The Greater Mysteries, which lasted eight days, were celebrated at Eleusis during the month of Boedromion (roughly mid-September to mid-October), and were open to women, slaves, and Greek-speaking foreigners, as well as to Athenian citizens. Present for the ritual were both first-time participants (*mystai*) and "watchers" (*epoptai*) who had been through the rite at least once before. After an initial purification, which included ritual bathing in the sea and the sacrifice of a piglet by each initiate, the mystai apparently fasted at home for a day and then gathered with the others to march from Athens to Eleusis. In this procession the priestesses carried baskets (*kistai*) containing "sacred things" which had been brought from Eleusis a few days earlier. At a bridge over the Kephisos river which marked the boundary between Athens and Eleusis, masked participants made obscene gestures and jokes as the *mystai* passed by. The final stages of the walk would have been completed after dark and by torch-light.

In the evening of the next day, the *mystai*, accompanied by the epoptai, were led by torch-light into the *telesterion*, a large "Hall of Mysteries," where the rest of the ceremony took place. The final stages of the rite were conducted by torch-light and were so secret that very little evidence has survived about them beyond the fact that they included "things said" (*legomena*), "things done" (*dromena*) and "things revealed" (*deiknumena*). The ceremony in the darkened telesterion seems to have included a sacrifice, the revelation of sacred objects, a "sacred encounter" between the priestess and the hierophant, (the "revealer of sacred things" who emerged at some point from a dark, inner chamber called the *anaktoron* where a great fire burned), and the participation of a boy called "the one initiated from the hearth." The role played by this boy is unknown, although a child cowering before two figures with torches is visible on a badly damaged relief depicting a scene from the rite. Finally, the hierophant struck a gong to call Kore up from the underworld, announced "the Mistress has given birth to a sacred boy,

Brimo the Brimos," and, in silence, revealed a cut blade of wheat. The meaning of these details has been interpreted variously but remains, like the rest of the rite, a mystery.

In the end, the *Hymn to Demeter* deserves to be seen as more than a combination of independent stock themes, or as a source for clues about the Eleusinian Mysteries, and its distinct treatment of Demeter and Persephone's story deserves serious attention in its own right. Ancient evidence attests to the existence of different versions of this story by Orpheus, Musaeus, and other poets. In these other versions, Demeter wanders the earth searching for her daughter and, disguised as an old woman, is taken in by the ruling family of Eleusis. She becomes the nurse of the queen's infant boy and attempts to make him immortal by placing him in a fire. When his mother discovers her doing this, the goddess becomes angry and kills the child in the fire. She then reveals her true identity and, after asking what has become of Persephone, she learns her daughter's fate from Triptolemos (and his brother) who witnessed the abduction. In return for this information and, in some versions, also for their hospitality, she rewards the inhabitants of Eleusis with the gift of agriculture, which Triptolemos teaches to the rest of mankind, and with the instruction of her sacred rites. In some accounts Demeter herself goes to the underworld to retrieve her daughter, and Persephone's return is linked closely to the delineation of regular seasons in the year. As told in these versions, the myth makes the theme of the seasons and the gift of agriculture central to the story.

This is not so in the Homeric hymn, which differs from the Orphic and other accounts in several important ways. After Zeus engineers a marriage for Hades which will link the upper and lower worlds, Demeter learns of Persephone's fate from the god Helios (and Hekate) and journeys to Eleusis with this knowledge. Her arrival at Eleusis is thus cast in a new light, as the goddess withdraws from the immortal sphere in anger at Zeus for arranging a marriage which will relegate Persephone to the world of the dead and remove her forever from the Olympian sphere. Perhaps as a direct challenge to Zeus' authority, Demeter then attempts to match his blurring of the line between mortal and divine by herself granting immortality to a human child. When her attempt fails she does not kill the child, but demands instead that the people of Eleusis build a temple to propitiate her anger. This temple provides her with a place to withdraw also from the world of men. During this second withdrawal she causes a famine, not mentioned in the other accounts, which not only starves mortals, but also deprives the gods of those sacrifices which define their existence. This famine wins a compromise from Zeus which allows Persephone to return from the world of the dead to the upper world for a portion of each year. The compromise ends Demeter's conflict with Zeus and resolves the tension between mortal and immortal spheres which the hymn's narrative has brought into prominence. The poem ends, not with the goddess' gift of agriculture, but with Demeter establishing a rite through which mankind can achieve their own kind of blessed state, even within the bounds of mortality (480-482).

Although the Homeric hymn is the earliest text we have for the myth of Demeter and Persephone, the tradition(s) preserved in later literary accounts or artistic representations may be just as old or even older than that of the hymn. The myth itself is rich enough to include all the varied elements discussed above, and each poet or tradition was free to combine those elements in different ways to emphasize one over another with each retelling of the story. So the motifs of hospitality, abduction, marriage the cycle of seasons, the challenge of one god's authority by another god, and even the tension between mortal and immortal spheres all coexist within the myth, like threads in a tapestry. The thread which appears most prominent, if any one does, will depend on the skill of the weaver and the eye of the beholder.

HYMN TO DEMETER

Demeter,° fair-haired, holy goddess, I begin to sing,
her and her slender-ankled daughter° whom Aidoneus°
seized, and loud-thundering, far-seeing Zeus granted it,°
without the knowledge of Demeter of the golden sword° and

1-11   As often in early hexameter, the first word in the poem names its
        subject, Demeter. In the Greek text, lines 1-11 set the scene for this
        hymn in one long sentence which juxtaposes the peaceful and
        unknowing innocence of Demeter and her daughter against the
        willfullness and raw power of Zeus and his brother. The collusion of
        the young girl's great-grandmother, Gaia, in this forced marriage
        seems initially troubling, although her consent replaces that of the
        absent Demeter and provides a hint of the ultimate reconciliation with
        which the hymn will end.

2a   Persephone, the daughter of Demeter and Zeus, is not actually named
        in the hymn until line 55. At line 8 she is called simply kore, "maiden,"
        a term by which she is worshipped in cult as the Maiden Goddess.

2b   Aidoneus is a lengthened form of the name Hades. The god of the
        underworld is called "lord of many," and "the one who receives
        many" (e.g. 9, 30) because all mortals eventually die and fall under his
        rule. Like Zeus, he is also called "son of Kronos" (e.g. 18).

3   This formula for Zeus' name combines the Homeric epithet "far- or
        wide-seeing" and the Hesiodic "loud-thundering" for the first time. It
        recurs three more times in the hymn.
        As Persephone's father, Zeus would appropriately have given her
        away in a lawful marriage, but the verb here ("give, grant") also
        indicates his power, as king of the gods, to allow Hades' abduction of
        Persephone. Line 9 suggests he not only granted the abduction but
        helped to plan it. In the Orphic and other versions of the myth, Zeus is
        a witness and sometimes a participant in the abduction. His granting
        of Persephone in marriage to Hades effects a formal link between
        Hades' realm of the dead and the upper world ruled by Zeus.
        In the Greek text, the word translated here (l.4) as "without the
        knowledge of" also indicates that Persephone was playing at some
        distance from Demeter. It is impossible to capture both senses with
        one word in English. The same word is used of Zeus, who is far away
        when his daughter calls on him for help at line 27.

4   Why Demeter should be connected with a golden sword here is not at all

---

splendid fruit,
as the girl was playing with the deep-bosomed daughters of
    Okeanos°   5
picking flowers, roses, and crocus, and beautiful violets
throughout the soft meadow, and irises, and hyacinth,
and the narcissus which Gaia° made grow as a trick for the
    blushing maiden,
pleasing the one who receives many, by the will of Zeus
— a flower shining marvelously, a wonder for all to see,   10
both immortal gods and mortal men.
From its root a hundred blooms had grown forth
and their fragrance was very sweet, and the whole broad
    heaven above
and all the earth laughed, and the salty swell of the sea.
Then, struck with wonder she reached out with both hands   15
to take the lovely toy. But the wide-pathed ground gaped open
along the plain of Nysa° where the lord who receives many
    sprang out

---

clear. The epithet elsewhere describes Apollo, Artemis, Zeus and others, although its precise meaning is not always certain. Lycophron (*Alex.* 153) calls Demeter "sword-bearer" in connection with her cult in Boiotia.

5   The daughters of Okeanos and Tethys are called *korai* (pl.), a term which means both "maidens" and "daughters," and which echoes Persephone's own cult title *Kore* ("maiden" e.g. line 8). In the *Theogony* (346-370) they are said to help Apollo raise young men to adulthood, but here the nymphs appear simply as youthful playmates for Persephone who lists some of them by name later in the hymn (418-424).

The theme of a young girl (or girls) being carried off while playing is traditional. Such stories usually include a description of (1) the maidens— postponed in this hymn until 418-424, (2) the location—usually in a meadow or by a spring, (3) their activities—singing, dancing, playing, picking flowers, (4) any male companions—absent here, and (5) one maiden who stands out among the rest. The scene of Nausikaä and her companions in the fifth book of the *Odyssey* may originally have belonged to this type, although the intrusion of Odysseus did not result in an abduction as Hades' entrance does in the hymn.

8   Gaia, the goddess of the earth, is the grandmother of Zeus and Hades, who joins their plot to abduct Persephone by providing the magical flower (the narcissus) which will open up the earth. At Eleusis, worshippers gathered spring flowers in celebration of Persephone's return, but their actions also recall the scene of her abduction.

17   The location of the mythical "plain of Nysa" is uncertain. One site in Caria bearing this name had a cult of Demeter, Kore and Pluto, but there is no clear connection with that cult and this hymn. In other myths, Nysa is the birthplace of Dionysos (see hymn 1).

with his immortal horses, the son of Kronos, worshipped under
    many names.°
He seized her against her will and on his golden chariot
carried her off wailing. And she cried aloud with a shrill voice,   20
calling on her father, the highest and best son of Kronos.
But no one either of the gods or mortal men
heard her cry, not even the olives with their splendid fruit.°

Only the youthful daughter of Persaios
heard from her cave, Hekate° of the shining veil,   25
and lord Helios, glorious son of Hyperion,°
as the maiden called her father, the son of Kronos. But he was far
    away
sitting apart from the gods in his temple where many pray,
receiving beautiful sacrifices from mortal men.
So her father's brother, lord of many, the one who receives many,°   30

---

18   Hades is "worshipped under many names" in part because no one
    wants to risk displeasing him by omitting his favorite title. The listing of
    many titles for any god or goddess is a regular feature of prayers for this
    reason. In the case of Hades, whose name no one wanted to speak aloud
    in case it brought bad luck, the different titles or epithets had an added
    advantage.

23   The significance of the olives here is unknown. As a regular feature of
    the landscape in Greece they may be mentioned simply to represent a
    power of nature, especially since they share with Demeter the epithet
    "with/of splendid fruit". Whether they should be personified (as
    goddesses of the olive trees) or we are to believe the olives themselves
    could hear remains a puzzle. Olive-trees, along with fig-trees, barley,
    wheat, and vines were cited as witnesses in the oath of young Athenian
    ephebes beginning military service (Tod 1933-1948, II 204.20).

25   Hekate, the daughter of Persaios and Asteriê, is the subject of her own
    hymn in Hesiod's *Theogony* (409-452), although she does not appear in
    Homer. Her worship apparently originated in Caria but must have been
    well-established in Greece by the time of the hymn. In the cult at Eleusis
    she was an attendant of Persephone and Demeter, and she functions in
    the hymn primarily as Demeter's companion, providing the information
    which leads Demeter to Helios and the discovery of her daughter's fate.
    Hekate occasionally also appears in vase-paintings depicting the myth
    of Persephone's abduction and return (fig. 1).

26   According to Hesiod (*Th.* 374) the sun god Helios was the son of Titans
    Hyperion and Theia (see genealogical chart); in Homer "Hyperion"
    generally occurs as an epithet of Helios. The sun is often a witness to
    what happens on earth, perhaps because of his superior vantage point
    in the sky (cf. *Il.* 3.277; *Od.* 11.109; h. *H.* 381).

30   In the Greek text, this line (= line 31) stands out as unusual and

son of Kronos, worshipped under many names, with his
    immortal horses
carried her off against her will at the prompting of Zeus.

As long as the goddess saw the earth and starry heaven
and the swift-flowing sea teeming with fish,
and the rays of the sun, and still hoped to see her devoted   35
mother and the race of the gods who are forever,
so long did hope charm her great mind, though she was grieving.°

But the mountain peaks and the depths of the sea rang
with her immortal voice, and her queenly mother heard her.
And a sharp grief took hold of Demeter in her heart, and
    with both hands   40
she tore the veil on her immortal hair,
and she cast her dark cloak down from both her shoulders,
and she rushed like a bird over the nourishing land and sea
searching. But no one either of gods or mortal men
was willing to tell her the truth, nor   45
did any of the birds come to her as a true messenger.

For nine days, then, over the earth queenly Deo°
roamed about, holding blazing torches in her hands,

---

noteworthy since it contains only three words, each an epithet beginning with the letter p. This piling up of epithets is more natural in the Greek than it sounds in English.

37   There may be a lacuna (a break in the text where one or more lines are missing) after this line since the narrative as it stands (67-68) seems to contradict lines 23-24. The sense of the missing text would be something like, "but when she was entering the gaping earth and realized that she was being carried down to the underworld, then indeed she despaired and cried out still more vehemently than before" (Richardson 1974: 161). Such an addition would supply both a mention of Persephone's second cry, which is heard by her mother (39), and her actual descent below the earth, a regular feature in other accounts of the myth and an important part of the cult at Eleusis. In any case, lines 33-37 imply what the lost lines might have made explicit: once Persephone entered the underworld she would not have been able to return to the upper world and would therefore have had no hope of seeing her mother (or the other gods) again.

47   Deo is probably a shortened form of Demeter. Her epithet, *potnia*, is translated here (and elsewhere) as "queenly," and in line 54 as "mistress." Neither English word quite captures the spirit of the Greek term, which conveys a sense of the august and holy power inherent in the goddess. For the nine day period, see below on line 50.

and she never tasted ambrosia or the sweet drink, nectar,°
as she grieved, nor did she wash her skin with water.°   50
But when indeed the tenth Dawn came bringing light,
Hekate, holding a torch in her hands, met her
and spoke to her, telling her the news,

"Mistress Demeter, bringer of seasons, giver of splendid gifts,
who of the heavenly gods or mortal men   55
seized Persephone and grieved your dear heart?
For I heard her voice but did not see with my eyes
who it was. I am telling you swiftly the whole truth."

So spoke Hekate. And the daughter of fair-haired Rhea°
did not answer her with speech, but darted off with her   60
swiftly, holding blazing torches in her hands.
And they came to Helios, who watches over both gods and men,
and they stood in front of his horses° and the shining goddess spoke.
"Helios, since you are a god, respect me as a goddess, if indeed
    I have ever cheered
your heart and spirit either by word or deed.   65
The maiden whom I bore, a sweet young flower, glorious in form —
I heard her wailing voice through the barren air
as if she were being forced, but I did not see her with my eyes.

49   In early epic poetry ambrosia was the regular food of the gods and nectar was their drink. Some later authors (including Alcman and Sappho) reverse the two. Both were thought to impart strength or immortality, and for this reason Demeter anoints the baby Demophoön with them at 237 (see 242n.).

50   In the cult at Eleusis "mystic dramas" were performed at night re-enacting Demeter's grief-stricken search for her daughter by torch-light. The rite apparently ended with the "tossing" of these torches in thanksgiving when Persephone was found. Similarly, the Eleusinian ritual also included a period of fasting and, perhaps, a prohibition against bathing before the festival. The nine-day period mentioned here may simply be conventional; this number is common in Homer and elsewhere (e.g. Apollo's plague at *Il.* 1.53; Leto's period of labor at the birth of Apollo in h. *Ap.* 91).

59   The Titans Rhea and Kronos had three daughters (Hestia, Demeter, Hera) and three sons (Poseidon, Hades, Zeus); see genealogical chart. Here the "daughter of Rhea" is Demeter.

63   Homer does not speak of a chariot of the Sun, although Dawn's chariot is mentioned at *Od.* 23.244. The convention that the sun drove a horse-drawn chariot across the sky is common in other mythologies, and a Greek vase from ca. 670-660 BC showing the sun god Helios with a horse appears to support the view that it was popular in early Greek myth as well.

But since you look down from the shining air with your rays
over all the earth and sea,   70
tell me truthfully of my dear child, if anywhere you have seen
who either of gods or even of mortal men, in my absence,
took her by force against her will and went away?"

So she spoke, and the son of Hyperion answered her,
"Lady Demeter, daughter of fair-haired Rhea,   75
you will know, for I revere you greatly and I pity you
as you grieve over your slender-ankled child. No one else
of the immortals is responsible except cloud-gathering Zeus,
who gave her to Hades, his own brother, to be called his
youthful wife. He seized her and with his horses   80
led her wailing loudly down to the misty gloom.
But, goddess, put a stop to your great mourning — you should not
hold such boundless grief this way in vain. The lord of many
is not an unfit son-in-law among the immortals, Aidoneus,
your own brother and born of the same seed. And as for honor, 85
he received his share when the three-fold division was made
        for the first time:°
he lives with those whose ruler he was allotted to be."
So speaking, he called to his horses, and at his shouting they
carried the swift chariot quickly like long-winged birds.

But a more terrible and savage grief came into Demeter's heart.° 90
Then, angered at the dark-clouded son of Kronos,
she avoided the assembly of the gods and lofty Olympos,
and went among the cities of men and their rich fields
softening her form° for a long while. No one of men

---

86   *Iliad* 15.189-92 describes how Zeus, Hades and Poseidon each received
      his own domain (the sky, the underworld, and the sea respectively) by
      lot. Hesiod preserves another tradition according to which the
      supreme rule and the power to distribute honor to the other gods went
      to Zeus at their insistence and that of Gaia after the battle between the
      Olympians and Titans (*Th.* 883-885).

90   Demeter's grief increases not because Hades is an unworthy son-in-
      law, but because she knows no return from the underworld is allowed,
      except to the messenger god Hermes. The marriage of the immortal
      Persephone becomes, in a very real sense, the girl's death. In her anger,
      Demeter withdraws from the immortal sphere herself and joins
      instead the world of mankind.

94   Demeter here literally "softens" or "effaces" her divine appearance to
      appear as an old woman so she will not be recognized. The theme of a
      disguised god wandering among men is common (e.g. Athena in the

and of deep-girded women recognized her when they
    looked at her,   95
until she came to the house of thoughtful Keleos,°
who at that time was a lord of fragrant Eleusis.°
And she sat grieving in her dear heart near the road
by the Parthenian well,° whence the citizens were
    accustomed to draw water,
in the shade where an olive bush grew above it.   100
She looked like a very old woman, one excluded from
childbearing and the gifts of garland-loving Aphrodite,
as are the nurses for the children of law-giving kings
and the housekeepers in their echoing homes.

And the daughters of Keleos, son of Eleusinos, saw her   105
as they came for the easily-drawn water, to carry it
in bronze pitchers to the dear home of their father,
four of them like goddesses having the bloom of youth,
Kallidike, and Kleisidike, and lovely Demo,
and Kallithoe, who was the eldest of them all.°   110

Odyssey) and it was not an uncommon practice to address strangers as though they were gods (e.g. Odysseus to Nausikaä *Od.* 6.149). This practice is explained by one of the suitors at *Od.* 17.483-487: "... the gods do take on all sorts of transformations, appearing / as strangers from elsewhere, and thus they range at large through the cities, / watching to see which men keep the laws, and which are violent." (translation by Lattimore)

96   Keleos was the son of Eleusinos, the eponymous hero of Eleusis. At 153-155 and 474-475 he is listed with other lords of the city, so it is not clear who among them was the chief ruler. He was a recipient of sacrifices at Eleusis where his wife and daughters also had a cult.

97   Eleusis is regularly called "fragrant," an epithet which looks forward to the sacrifices which were made there in Demeter's cult. Its use here, before the establishment of that cult in the myth, is formulaic.

99   The location of the Parthenian ("Maiden") well remains disputed. Some say this well is the same as one called Kallichoron ("Beautiful chorus") which was near the entrance of the Eleusinian sanctuary (and is still visible today). According to Pausanias (1.38.6), the Kallichoron was the spot where the Eleusinian women danced and sang in honor of the goddess. As Richardson (1974: 326) notes, the double name of the well would make sense if there were *choruses* of *maidens* around it. See 270-272n.

110   In other versions of the myth there are only three daughters whose names vary according to the source, (e.g. in the Orphic hymn Kalliope, Kleisdike, and Damonassa fetch water, with the queen as a fourth companion). Pausanias (1.38.3), citing Homer and Pamphos (a writer of hymns), names Diogeneia, Pammerope, and Saisara. While these names

They did not know her; gods are hard for mortals to recognize.
But standing near, they addressed her with winged words,°
"Who are you, old woman, of men born long ago? Where are you
    from?
Why have you wandered away from the city and do not approach
the houses? There, in the shady halls, are women   115
the same age as you and younger ones,
who would welcome you both in word and in deed."

So they spoke, and the queenly goddess answered,
"Dear children, whoever you are of tender women,
greetings; I will tell you my story. Surely it is not unfitting   120
to tell you the truth, since you ask.
Doso° is my name, for my queenly mother gave it to me.
Now from Crete over the broad back of the sea
I have come, unwilling, but by brute force
pirate men carried me off against my will. Then they   125
landed in their swift ship at Thorikos,° where the women
set foot on the shore all together and the men
prepared a meal by the stern-cables of the ship.
But my heart was not longing for the sweet evening meal,
and, starting off secretly through the dark land,   130
I fled my arrogant masters, so they would not sell me,
whom they had not bought, and have enjoyment of the price
    paid for me.°
So I have come wandering here, and I have no idea
what land this is and what men live here.

may belong to local legend, those in the Demeter hymn are more likely invented by the poet, especially since the repeated k and l sounds seemed designed for poetic effect. The meanings of the names (e.g. Kallidike "Beautiful justice") are probably not significant here; Demo ("People"), which is used elsewhere of Demeter may have been chosen to stress the future connection between the goddess and this family (cf. the note on her brother Demophoön at 234).

112   On "winged words" see h. *Aph.* 184n.

122   Like Odysseus, Demeter tells a false tale about herself to protect her true identity. The name Doso ("I will give") is an appropriate pseudonym for the goddess who gives crops to mankind. The inclusion of Crete is a common feature in tales of this sort (e.g. *Od.* 13.256, 14.199, 19.172; h. *Ap.* 469), as is the capture by pirates (e.g. *Od.* 14.334, 15.427; h. 7.6).

126   At the site of Thorikos, south of Athens on the north-east coast of Attica, are the remains of a 5th-century BC cult building which may have been dedicated to Demeter and Persephone and used for mystery rites like those of Eleusis.

131-132 The Greek here is as awkward as the English.

But may all who have their homes on Olympos grant   135
you men for husbands and children to bear
just as parents wish; but in turn, maidens, pity me°
. . . .
seriously, dear children, to whose house should I go,
a man's or woman's, in order that I may perform for them
eagerly those tasks which are fitting for an old woman?   140
Holding a new-born child in my arms
I would nurse him well and watch over the house
and make the master's bed in the innermost part
of the well-built chamber and I would oversee the women's work."

So spoke the goddess, and at once the unmarried maiden
answered her,   145
Kallidike, most beautiful of the daughters of Keleos,
"Dear mother, we mortals endure the gifts of the gods by necessity,
even though we are grieved, for indeed they are much stronger.°
But I will give you this advice clearly and name
the men who have great power of authority here   150
and are preeminent among the people, and they protect
the towers of the city with their counsels and straight judgements.
They are Triptolemos,° shrewd in counsel, and Dioklos
and Polyxeinos and blameless Eumolpos
and Dolichos and our own brave father,   155
who all have wives to manage affairs in the house.

---

137   A lacuna occurs here in the text. Similar breaks occur at lines 211 and
      236 which, like line 137, fall at the end of the manuscript page.
      Whatever else is missing here, the sense of the existing text requires a
      verb asking for the information detailed in 138.
148   This sentiment is common in ancient Greek thought, e.g. Achilles
      speech to Priam at the end of the *Iliad* (24.518ff.) or Nausikaä to
      Odysseus at *Od.* 6.187-190, and is repeated by Metaneira at 216-217.
      The opposite view, that mortals are responsible for their own actions,
      is argued by Zeus at *Od.* 1.32-43. Cf. h. *Dem.* 256-258, with note.
153-155 Triptolemos became an important hero in later Athenian legend,
      which said that he received the gift of grain from Demeter and was
      sent out by her to teach the art of agriculture to mankind. Scenes of his
      departure in a chariot first appear ca. 550-525 B.C. and by ca. 450-430
      BC he appears as a boy on the "Grand Relief" at Eleusis, perhaps
      replacing Demophoön (see on line 234) as Demeter's charge in the
      myth. In Apollodorus (1.5.1) he is the eldest son of Keleos and
      Metaneira. The derivation of his name is unsure, but ancient
      etymology connected it with the Greek word for "plough": "Thrice-
      ploughed" or "God of the triple ploughing."

Not one of these women at first sight would exclude you
from the house, dishonoring your appearance,
but they will receive you, for indeed you are godlike.
But if you wish, wait, so we may go to our father's   160
house and tell our mother, deep-girded Metaneira,
all these things right through, in the hope that she may bid you
come to our house and not search out the homes of others.
Her only son is being raised in the well-built hall,
born late, much prayed for and a joy.   165
If you should nurse him and he should reach the measure of his
     youth,
easily would any of the tender women, seeing you,
feel envy, such payment would she give you for raising him."

So she spoke, and the goddess nodded her head, and they,
walking proudly,
carried the shining vessels full of water.   170
Soon they came to the great house of their father, and quickly told
their mother what they had seen and heard. And she bid them
to go quickly and invite her to come for a boundless wage.
Like deer or heifers in the season of spring
leap along the meadow, satisfying their hearts with food,   175
so they, holding up the folds of their lovely garments,
darted along the low-lying road, and their hair

Dioklos (called Diokles at 474 and 477), was a Megarian hero whom
later Megarian legend said was a king of Eleusis driven out of that city
by Theseus. This detail points to the domination of Megara over
Eleusis before Athenian influence became prominent. He received
sacrifices with other heroes at Eleusis.

Polyxeinos ("Entertaining many guests") was also included among
the heroes who received sacrifices at Eleusis, but nothing else is
known of him. His name appears elsewhere as an epithet of Hades.

Eumolpos ("Good singer") held an important position in the cult as
the eponymous father of the family of priests (*Eumolpidai*) who spoke
(sang?) the sacred words of the rite. He is credited as founder of the
Mysteries in several sources, and is identified in some as the son of
Musaeus, a mythical singer closely related to the Thracian Orpheus.
Euripides, in the lost play *Erechtheus*, refers to another legend of his
birth in which he was thrown into the sea by his mother (Chione), and
rescued by Poseidon to be raised by the Ethiopians and become a king
of Thrace. Different versions of the myth in the hymn were ascribed to
the poets Orpheus, Musaeus, and Eumolpos.

Dolichos had a temple outside the Eleusinian sanctuary, but is not
otherwise an important figure. In some later sources he is called a son
of Triptolemos.

streamed about their shoulders like a crocus flower.°

They found the glorious goddess near the road where they had
    left her
before, and they led her to the dear house   180
of their father. She went behind with grief in her heart
and her head covered, and her dark robe
swirled around the goddess' slender feet.

Soon they came to the home of Keleos, cherished by Zeus,
and they went through the colonnade to where their queenly
    mother   185
sat by a pillar of the strongly-built roof
holding her child, her young offspring, in her lap. They ran to her,
but the goddess stood on the threshold, and her head
touched the roof-beam, and she filled the doorway with a divine
    radiance.°
Reverence and awe and pale fear seized Metaneira.   190
And she yielded her chair and bade her sit.°
But Demeter, bringer of seasons, giver of splendid gifts,
was unwilling to sit on the shining chair.

---

178   The description of the maidens, with robes held up and their yellow
hair falling loose, is in stark contrast to that of the veiled Demeter
whose dark robe trails on the ground (182-184). Since the combination
of the trailing robe and free-flowing hair is often connected with cult
practices, some have detected in this scene a reflection of the cult at
Eleusis. If so, the daughters of Keleos act in the hymn as the
prototypes of the Eleusinian priestesses who, also dressed in long
robes, with their hair unbound, would have led the initiates in the
ritual procession.

189   When gods or goddesses assume a disguise to visit men on earth, they
often reveal themselves either at their entrance (e.g. *Il.* 4.75) or, more
commonly, at their departure (e.g. *Od.* 1.319). Such revelations, or
epiphanies, are characterized by (1) the deity's supernatural size, (2) a
divine radiance, often accompanied by a divine fragrance, (3) the awe
and fear inspired in the onlookers. In spite of these very signs in 188-
190, Demeter is evidently *not* recognized as a god until her second
epiphany at 275-280; cf. Aphrodite's appearances to Anchises in the
Hymn to Aphrodite (84-85, 171-190).

191-210 The following passage is a typical scene showing the proper treatment
of a guest: the offer of a seat of honor, food and drink and, only
afterwards, an inquiry as to the stranger's identity. At the same time it
also provides a mythic explanation (*aition*) for some elements of the
ritual at Eleusis (1) **ritual purification**—expressed here by Demeter's
sitting, veiled and in silence, on the fleece (194-201), (2) **fasting and**

She stayed silent, her beautiful eyes downcast,
until devoted Iambe° set out for her   195
a well-pieced seat and threw over it a silver-white fleece.
Then sitting down, she held her veil before her with her hands.°
For a long time she sat on the chair speechless in her grief,
nor did she greet anyone by word or gesture,
but unsmiling, tasting no food or drink,   200
she sat wasting away with longing for her deep-girded daughter,
until devoted Iambe, intervening with jokes
and many jests, moved the holy lady
to smile and laugh and have a propitious heart;°
indeed in later times too she used to please her in her moods.   205

Metaneira offered her a cup filled with honey-sweet wine,
but she refused it, for she said it was not right
to drink the red wine. But she bid Metaneira to give her
a drink of barley-meal and water mixed with fresh pennyroyal.

---

    abstention from food (200, 206-208), (3) ritual jesting, here in the form
    of an obscene joke by Iambe (202-205), and (4) kykeon, the mixture of
    barley and water.
195   Iambe is the eponym for iambic meter, the regular rhythm used for
    blame poetry and comic jesting or insults. This meter may originally
    have been connected with religious contexts and was often
    accompanied by dancing. Aristophanes' *Frogs* (396ff.) provides a
    description of the sort of scene which might have taken place in the
    ritual at Eleusis with a procession of the chorus (initiates) and iambic
    jesting. The details of the ritual at Eleusis are not fully known.
    In the Orphic version of the myth, Iambe's place is taken by Baubo, the
    queen of Eleusis, who induces Demeter to laugh, apparently by lifting
    her skirt to expose herself. See 204n. below.
196-197 Both written and pictorial evidence indicates that a preliminary
    ceremony in which the veiled initiate sat on a skin-covered stool was a
    regular part of the ritual. In the hymn Demeter takes the part of the
    initiate in this *thronôsis* (sitting ceremony).
204   The hymnist is not specific about what Iambe actually says or does, but
    the parallel with Baubo (and many similar figures in other myths),
    suggests her jokes were obscene. This kind of sexual jesting (*aischrologia*)
    was an especially typical element of festivals to Demeter and to
    Dionysos, both deities associated with fertility.
    In the present context, the rude jokes help relieve Demeter's grief over
    the loss of her daughter (cf. Loki's obscenities which distract Skadi from
    his grief over his father's death in Norse mythology), while at the same
    time providing a mythic *aition* for the Eleusinian ritual. The hymnist
    thus weaves together the two apparently distinct parts of his story.

And she, having made the potion, gave it to the goddess as she
    had asked.
Taking it to show respect, the great mistress Deo°   210
. . . .
and among them well-girded Metaneira began to speak,
"Greetings, lady, since I expect you are not from base parents,
but good ones; reverence is in your eyes
and grace, as if you were born from law-giving kings.   215
But we mortals endure the gifts of the gods by necessity
even though we are grieved, for a yoke lies on our neck.
But now, since you have come here, whatever I have will be
    yours.
Nurse this child for me whom the immortals bestowed on me
late-born and beyond my hopes, though I wished for him
    so often.   220
If you should raise him and he should reach the measure of his
    youth,
surely any of the tender women, seeing you, would
feel envy, such payment will I give you for raising him."

---

210   The potion (*kykeon*) described here was a variation on the simple
        mixture of grain, liquid and herbs which was often given to visitors:
        Patroklos and Nestor drink a mixture of wine, cheese and barley in the
        Iliad (11.624-641), while Kirke offers Odysseus' men a similar potion
        containing honey and magical drugs as well (*Od.* 10.234-236). Later
        sources indicate the drink came to be used by poor or country people,
        and sometimes also for medicinal purposes.
        The *kykeon* was also the drink taken by participants after their period
        of fasting in the initiation ritual at Eleusis For this reason,
        commentators usually understand the phrase translated here as "to
        show respect" as meaning "for the sake of the rite." But Demeter's
        actions at this point could hardly be motivated by a rite which has not
        yet been established (at 273-274 Demeter says clearly that she will
        establish her rites *after* a temple has been built to propitiate her). The
        key word here (*hosie*) comes to refer, in later Greek, to things done
        according to divine law, and thus to "ritual," but here it more likely
        refers to the proper respect shown one another by host and guest in
        the relationship of guest-friendship. Demeter's refusal to drink the wine
        offered previously may be explained by her unwillingness to drink wine
        while in a state of mourning, just as Achilles refused to bathe until the
        body of his friend Patroklos had been buried. In order not to offend the
        honor of her hostess, Demeter does accept a more modest drink in place
        of the wine and, whatever else is missing in the lacuna (probably of two
        lines) following 210, Metaneira's next words make it clear that Demeter
        has indeed proved herself civilized by these actions.

Fair-wreathed Demeter answered her in turn,
"and to you many greetings, lady, and may the gods grant you
    good things.   225
Happily will I take your son as you bid.
I will raise him and, nor do I expect, a spell or the undercutter
will harm him through the ignorance of his nurse.
For I know an antidote far stronger than the herb-cutter,
and I know a good safeguard against baneful attacks."°   230
So she spoke and took the child to her fragrant bosom
in her immortal hands, and his mother rejoiced in her heart.

So the splendid son of thoughtful Keleos,
Demophoön,° whom well-girded Metaneira bore,
she nursed in the halls, and he grew like a god   235
not eating grain, nor sucking [his mother's milk].°
. . . . [by day] Demeter
used to anoint him with ambrosia as if he had been born from a
    god,
breathing on him sweetly and holding him to her bosom.
But night after night she used to bury him in the force of the fire,
    like a firebrand,°
in secret from his dear parents. And to them it was a great
    marvel   240
how he kept growing before his time and how he had become
    like the gods to look at.

---

230   The Greek word for "spell" and "attack" in these lines is the same, and implies an attack of pain caused by magic. The meaning of "undercutter" is not clear; one conjecture links it with a worm said to cause toothaches, while another suggests it is a poisonous root. Demeter's speech here is carefully vague and, in the Greek, is phrased as a magic incantation itself would be.

234   Demophoön's name, "Shining for the people," sounds like an invention by the poet (cf. his sister, Demo, at 109). It does not appear in art or in inscriptions from Eleusis and, in later versions of the story, Triptolemos takes the place of Demophoön. In some versions, the child is killed in the fire.

236   Once again a line has been lost from the text, probably (again) at the foot of the manuscript page. The angled brackets in the translation suggest the sense of the lost words.

239   Many parallels for this story exist both in Greek literature and other sources, e.g. Isis and the son of the king of Byblos (Plutarch, Isis and Osiris 15). Apollodorus (3.13.6) tells of Thetis' attempt to make Achilles immortal, also by hiding him in fire at night and anointing him with ambrosia by day. In that story the baby's father, Peleus, intervenes before she can protect Achilles' ankle bone. Apollonius

And she would have made him ageless and immortal,°
if well-girded Metaneira in her foolishness
had not watched all night long from her fragrant chamber
and seen her. But she cried out and struck both thighs,   245
afraid for her child, and blindness covered her mind.
Wailing she spoke winged words,
"My child, Demophoön, the stranger buries you
in a great fire and brings me sorrow and wretched pain."

So she spoke, weeping, and the shining goddess heard her.   250
In anger at her, fair-wreathed Demeter
with her immortal hands snatched from the fire
the dear child, whom Metaneira had borne in the halls beyond
     her hopes,
and thrust him away from her to the ground, terribly
     angry in her heart.
At the same time she spoke to well-girded Metaneira,   255
"Humans are foolish and without the sense to know their
     destiny
ahead of time, when good comes, or evil,
and you too were hopelessly blinded by your own folly.°

Rhodius (4.869ff.) preserves an account of the same story which is very
close to the description in the Demeter hymn and may have been
modelled on it (or on another account also known to the hymnist). In that
version, Apollonius explains that the fire will burn away Achilles' mortal
parts (869-870), while the ambrosia will make him immortal (871-872); see
next note.

242   The hymn gives no reason for Demeter's wish to make Demophoön
immortal. Some have argued that, having lost her own daughter through
the girl's marriage to the god of the dead, she wishes to replace her with a
male child who will not be lost to her through marriage. Others have seen
a motive of revenge leading Demeter either to deprive Hades of a mortal
life owed to him, by making Demophoön deathless, or to defy Zeus
himself by "producing" a male to challenge his authority. While her
attempt to grant immortality to a mortal does challenge the natural order
in a general way, the tone and focus of the hymn suggest an additional
motive: that in her grief, Demeter wants simply to ensure that a mortal
mother, who has showed her kindness, will not suffer the pain she has
herself suffered through the loss of a child. This benevolence toward
mankind lies at the heart of the mysteries she will eventually offer to all.
For the use of ambrosia to impart immortality or divine strength, cf. h. *Ap.*
123-25, where the baby Apollo is fed nectar and ambrosia by Themis. In
the *Hymn to Aphrodite* (220ff.) ambrosia makes Tithonos immortal, but not
ageless.

258   Like Zeus at *Od.* 1.32-43, Demeter complains that humans don't have the

May the oath of the gods, the pitiless water of the Styx,° know
that I would have made your dear child immortal and ageless   260
all his days, and I would have granted him unfailing honor.
Now there is no way for him to avoid death and a mortal fate.
But unfailing honor will be his forever, because
he climbed up on my knees and slept in my arms.
And in due season, as the years revolve for him,   265
the children of the Eleusinians will always wage war
and bitter strife with each other all their days.°
 I am Demeter holder of honor, who is the greatest
help and joy to immortals and mortals.
But come, let all the people build me a great temple   270
and below it an altar, beneath the acropolis and its sheer wall
overlooking Kallichoron on a jutting hill.°
I myself will teach my rites, so that hereafter
you may propitiate my heart by performing them reverently."
So speaking, the goddess changed her size and form,   275
thrusting away old age. Beauty breathed around and about her,°
and a lovely scent spread from her fragrant
robes, and from the goddess' immortal skin a light
shone far off, and her golden hair spread down over
  her shoulders,
and the well-built house was filled with a bright light, as
  if from lightning.   280

She went out of the house and at once Metaneira's knees went
  slack

---

  sense to recognize or accept the favors of the gods when they come. This inability to recognize good or evil at its appearance is characteristic of humans in Greek literature.

259 The Styx ("the hated one") was a river in the Underworld which became the most powerful oath of the gods. See h. *Ap.* 85n.

267 These lines refer to a ritual mock battle performed at Eleusis in honor of Demophoön, either at a separate festival for him or as part of the Mysteries. Whether the origin of this "war" lay in a historical battle remains uncertain.

272 Archaeologists have found Classical remains of a temple, the Telesterion, on a terraced slope below the acropolis at Eleusis There is also evidence of earlier buildings on the same site from the Mycenaean and early Archaic periods, but whether either served a religious function has not been proved.

276 Demeter's second epiphany is unambiguous and more fully detailed than her first (188-190), but here too her appearance and stature change, and she gives off a radiance and fragrance which inspire fear

and for a long time she remained speechless and completely
forgot
to pick up her only son from the floor.
His sisters heard his piteous crying
and leapt down from their well-spread beds; then one   285
picked up the child in her arms and put him to her breast,
another stirred up the fire, and another rushed on tender feet
to rouse their mother from her fragrant chamber.
Gathering around him they washed him as he struggled°
though they handled him lovingly. But his heart was not
soothed,   290
for indeed inferior nurses and attendants were holding him.

All night long, shaking with fear, they propitiated
the glorious goddess° and, as soon as dawn appeared,
they told mighty Keleos truthfully,
what Demeter, the goddess of the lovely garland, had
commanded.   295
Then he called the people from all districts to an assembly,
and ordered them to build a rich temple to fair-haired Demeter
and an altar on the jutting hill.

They obeyed at once and heeded his words,
and they built it as he had ordered, and it grew by the decree
of the goddess.   300
When they had finished and quit from their toil,
each man went home. But golden-haired Demeter
remained sitting there, apart from all the blessed ones,
wasting away with longing for her deep-girded daughter.
And she caused a most terrible and savage year for men°   305

and awe in those around her. These reactions are the same as those
aroused in the initiates during the later cult of the goddess.

289   The Greek verb here (*aspairo*) is used in Homer always of the dying, who
       are gasping out their last breath. It is possible that the hymnist intended
       an allusion here to the tradition in which the baby dies in the fire.
       Equally, he may have wanted to emphasize the pain of Demophoön's
       removal from the immortal sphere and the consequent inevitability of
       his death.

293   This night-long ritual of propitiation may reflect an historical part of the
       rite at Eleusis conducted by women apart from the men. If so, it may
       have included the maidens' dance around the well mentioned earlier. A
       similar night ritual, the *pannychis*, was also part of the women's festival,
       the Thesmophoria

305-333 As lines 303-304 make clear, the loss of Persephone, not the foolishness
       of the Eleusinians, is the cause of Demeter's grief and anger. Just as

on the much-nourishing land, and the earth did not sprout
any seed, for fair-wreathed Demeter buried it.
Many curved ploughs did the oxen drag in the soil in vain,
and much white barley fell to no avail on the earth.
And now she would have destroyed the whole race of
    mortal men   310
with painful famine, and she would have deprived
the Olympians of the splendid honor of gifts and sacrifices,
if Zeus had not noticed and pondered in his heart.

First he roused golden-winged Iris° to summon
fair-haired Demeter, lovely in form.   315
So he spoke,° and she obeyed Zeus, the dark-clouded son
    of Kronos,
and she ran swiftly on her feet between earth and heaven.
And she came to the city of fragrant Eleusis
and found the dark-cloaked Demeter in her temple,
and she addressed her with winged words,   320
"Demeter, father Zeus, who has unfailing knowledge,
    calls you
to join the race of the gods who are forever.
So come, do not let my message from Zeus be unaccomplished."

Thus she spoke, begging, but the other's heart was not
    persuaded.
Then again the father sent, one after another, all the blessed   325
gods who are forever and, coming in succession,
they kept calling her and offering many beautiful gifts,

Poseidon stirred up a sea-storm in anger at Odysseus, Demeter here punishes both mankind and the gods (310-313) by withholding from them those things which lie in her domain: grain and wheat. The theme of famine brought about by the withdrawal of a god (through anger or other causes) is common in many cultures. The suffering of mortals here is a necessary result, but not a primary purpose, of Demeter's plan to punish the gods by making sacrifices to them impossible.

314   Iris, a granddaughter of Okeanos, was the personification of the rainbow which stretched from sky to earth and, as such, was a natural messenger of the gods (cf. h. *Ap.* 102). Like other winged figures in Archaic art, she was portrayed with wings on her ankles.

316   The use of this Homeric formula, which regularly follows a direct speech, seems odd here since Zeus' actual words to Iris are not given. Similarly, Iris' speech to Demeter at 320-322 ends abruptly ("But come, ...") without giving the details of Zeus' message. In Homer, Zeus' original speech to Iris would probably have been reported in full and repeated again by Iris to Demeter.

and whatever honors she might choose among the immortals.°
But no one could persuade her mind or intent
since she was angry in her heart, and she steadfastly spurned
    their words.   330
She said she would never set foot on
fragrant Olympos, nor sprout seed from the earth
until she saw with her own eyes her fair-faced daughter.

When loud-thundering, far-seeing Zeus heard this,
he sent Argeiphontes° of the golden wand to Erebos°   335
in order to persuade Hades with gentle words,
and bring back from the misty gloom to the light among the gods
holy Persephone, so that her mother, seeing her
with her own eyes, might cease from her anger.
And Hermes did not disobey, but leaving his Olympian seat   340
he rushed quickly down to the hiding-places of earth.

He found the lord inside his house
sitting on a bed with his shy wife
very reluctant in her longing for her mother, [and ...
....]°   345
Standing near, the mighty Argeiphontes said,
"Dark-haired Hades, lord of those who have died,
father Zeus bids me bring noble Persephone
out of Erebos among the gods, so that her mother,
seeing her with her own eyes, might cease from her anger   350
and her terrible wrath at the immortals. For she is devising
    a great plan

---

328   Like Agamemnon's offers to Achilles through various messengers in
      book nine of the *Iliad*, Zeus' offer of gifts and honors cannot soothe the
      anger of Demeter.
335a Argeiphontes is another name for Hermes (see h. *H.* 73). While
      Hermes and Iris both served as messengers of the gods to men, only
      Hermes travelled to the underworld.
335b Erebos ("Darkness") is another common name for the underworld. In
      Hesiod's *Theogony* (123-125) Erebos and his sister, Nyx ("Night"), were
      the offspring of Chaos, who mate with each other to produce their
      opposites, Aither ("Brightness") and Day. See genealogical chart.
344-345 The Greek in the manuscript here does not make sense and to date
      has not been emended satisfactorily. The original text may have
      continued the image of the unhappy Persephone, but the lines as
      transmitted and emended suggest that "Demeter, far away,
      contemplates a plan in revenge for the deeds of the blessed gods." The
      corruption may be linked to mention of Demeter's plan at line 351.

to destroy the feeble tribes of earth-born men
by burying the seed under the earth and utterly destroying
    the honors
of the immortals.° She is terribly angry and does not mingle
with the gods, but aloof in her fragrant temple   355
she sits, dwelling in the rocky city of Eleusis."

So he spoke, and Aidoneus, lord of those below the earth, smiled
with his eyebrows, nor did he disobey the commands of Zeus
    the king.
Quickly he ordered thoughtful Persephone,
"Go, Persephone, to your dark-robed mother,   360
keeping a gentle spirit and temper in your heart,
and do not be too despondent beyond the others.
Among the immortals I shall not be an unfitting husband,
    you know,
since I am father Zeus' own brother. And when you are here°
you shall be queen of all that lives and moves,   365
and you shall have the greatest honors among the immortals.
And there will always be punishment for those who have
    wronged you,
those who do not propitiate your spirit with sacrifices,
performing holy rites and offering proper gifts."

So he spoke, and wise Persephone rejoiced,   370
and jumped up quickly in delight. But he himself,
in secret, gave her the honey-sweet seed of a pomegranate
    to eat,
peering around him,° so she would not remain all her days
again with revered Demeter of the dark cloak.

---

354   If no crops grow on earth, no sacrifices can be made to honor the gods.

364   The Greek is ambiguous here and has been interpreted to mean either "while you are here [in the underworld with me]" or "when you are there [in the upper world, with your mother]." Those who accept the latter view see in Hades' speech a reference to Persephone's powers in the underworld (367-369), on earth (365), and in heaven (366). See 400n. below.

374   The meaning of this phrase is not certain, but it seems to reinforce the secrecy of Hades' action: he peers around to make sure no one (especially Hermes?) is watching as he slips the seed into her mouth. In other versions she eats three seeds (Ovid *Fasti* 4.607), or seven seeds which she herself picked from a tree in a garden (Ovid *Met.* 5.535).

    The pomegranate was associated with blood and death, perhaps because of the red color of its fruit; Clement of Alexandria records the

Then the ruler of many, Aidoneus, harnessed   375
his immortal horses in front of the golden chariot.
And she mounted the chariot, and beside her the strong
    Argeiphontes,
taking the reins and whip in his own hands,
hastened from the halls, and the two horses flew readily.
Swiftly they finished their long journey, and neither the sea   380
nor the water of rivers nor the grassy glens
nor the mountain-peaks held back the onrush of the
    immortal horses,
but above these they cut through the high air as they went.
Hermes brought them to a stop where fair-wreathed
    Demeter waited
in front of the fragrant temple. Seeing them,   385
she darted forth like a maenad° down a mountain
    shaded with trees.
And Persephone, for her part,° when she saw the beautiful eyes
of her mother, left the chariot and horses, and jumped down
to run to her, and fell upon her, embracing her neck.

And as Demeter was still holding her dear child in her arms,   390
suddenly her mind suspected a trick, and she shrank back,
    terribly afraid,
stopping her embrace, and at once questioned her.
"My child, when you were below you didn't eat any
food, did you? Speak up, don't hide it, so that we may
    both know.

---

belief that the pomegranate tree sprang from the blood of Dionysos Zagreus at his death. But it was also associated with fertility and marriage, and so here probably symbolizes the marriage of Persephone and Hades, acting symbolically for the feast which would have ended a formal marriage ceremony between the two.

The notion that eating any food in the underworld would prevent one from returning to the land of the living is common in many cultures; there are similar stories from Finland, South Africa, New Zealand, the Sioux Indians and elsewhere. The flower of the Lotos-Eaters, which causes Odysseus' men to forget their own return home in Homer's *Odyssey*, probably belongs to this world of the folk-tale.

386   A maenad was a female worshipper of Dionysos, characterized by her frenzied behavior, which included running wildly in the mountains and fields as if intoxicated or in a state of madness. See fig. 10.

387   There is a tear in the manuscript at this point so that only the first few words in each line from 387-401 remain. The translation here accepts supplements by early editors of the text which are only "best guesses" at the lost material. Text has also been lost at 462-479 due to the same tear.

For, if not, you will come up from dreadful Hades,   395
and live with me and your father, the dark-clouded son
     of Kronos,
being honored by all the immortals.
But if you ate anything, you will go back beneath the depths
     of the earth
and live there for a third part of the seasons every year,
but for two parts with me and the other immortals.°   400
And whenever the earth blossoms with fragrant spring-flowers
of every sort, then from the misty gloom
you will rise up again, a great wonder for gods and mortal men.°
With what trick did the mighty lord who receives many
     deceive you?"°

And beautiful Persephone addressed her again in response,   405
"Then, mother, I will tell you everything truthfully.

400   Many versions of the myth have Persephone spending six months each
       below and above the ground (e.g. Ovid *Met.* 5.564ff.) while others agree
       with the division of four and eight months made here (e.g. Apollodorus
       1.5.3). While the oldest division of the year was evidently into winter and
       summer, the existence of three seasons was already accepted in Homer
       and Hesiod. It has been noted that the three-fold division of the seasons in
       the hymn recapitulates the three-fold division of the cosmos into heaven,
       earth, and underworld and, perhaps, the tripartite division of
       Persephone's powers in those spheres (cf. 364n.).

401-403 Although the myth of Persephone/Kore is a good example of a nature
       allegory in which her descent to the underworld represents the planting
       of the seed, and her return the growth of the grain in the spring, it does
       not accurately represent the agricultural year in the Mediterranean area.
       In Greece, grain is sown in the autumn, germinates under the earth only
       for a few weeks, then sprouts and grows steadily through the winter. This
       discrepancy led one scholar of Greek religion, Martin P. Nilsson, to
       another interpretation which equates Kore's time in the underworld with
       the storage of seed grain in underground granaries during the dry
       summer months, and her return with the retrieval of the seed when the
       rains of autumn arrive. However consistent with fact, this interpretation is
       unlikely to be valid since, for the Greeks themselves, the association of
       Persephone's return with the fertility of the earth at spring-time was
       fundamental to the myth. It is important, however, to note that
       Persephone's return will not *cause* the earth to bloom, but that the flowers
       of spring will precede her arrival. See introductory note to hymn.

404   The trick referred to here is probably Hades' deceit in forcing Persephone
       to eat the pomegranate, not, as some have argued, his deceit in abducting
       Persephone (which she describes at 414ff.). Although Demeter began by
       asking Persephone *if* she had eaten anything in the underworld (393), it is
       clear that she already feared Hades' deceit (391) and, after explaining the
       consequences of having eaten in the underworld (395-403), she comes full

When the swift° messenger, Argeiphontes, came to me
from my father, Kronios,° and the other heavenly gods,
and told me to go from Erebos so that, seeing me with your
    own eyes,
you would cease from your anger at the immortals and
    your dreadful wrath,   410
at once I jumped up in joy. But Hades secretly
put in my mouth the seed of a pomegranate, honey-sweet food,
and, though I was unwilling, he made me eat it by force.
How, having snatched me up according to the shrewd plan
    of Kronos' son,
my father, he departed carrying me below the depths
    of the earth,   415
I will tell and recount everything you ask.
We were all playing in the delightful meadow,
Leucippe,° Phaino, Elektra, Ianthe,
Melite, Iache, Rhodeia, Kallirhoe,
Melobosis, Tyche, Okyrhoe, with a face like a flower,   420
Chryseis, Ianeira, Akaste, Amete,
Rhodope, Plouto, lovely Kalypso,
Styx, Ourania, charming Galaxaura,
Pallas, who rouses battle, and Artemis, rainer of arrows,
and we were picking lovely flowers with our hands: 425
soft crocus mingled with irises and hyacinth
and rose-blooms and lilies, a wonder to see,
and narcissus, which the wide earth grew like a crocus.°
And I began to pick it with joy, but the earth below
gave way, and the mighty lord who receives many sprang
    out from it.   430
He carried me off below the earth in his golden chariot,
much against my will, and I cried aloud with my voice.

circle to ask about the trick as a certainty. Thus, after promising to tell
the whole story (406), Persephone answers this question first (407-413)
before going on to describe the rest of her ordeal (414ff.).

407   For "swift messenger" see h. H. 3n. The translation here follows the text
      of the papyrus which was altered in the later manuscript, probably
      when the gloss "Hermes" supplanted "Argeiphontes" in the text.
408   Kronios = Zeus.
418-424 Hesiod lists 41 daughters of Okeanos in his catalog (Th. 349ff.), but
      Persephone mentions only 16 here. Some of those listed here are not in
      the Hesiodic catalogue (e.g. Leucippe, Phaino, Tyche).
428   The meaning of this phrase is not certain, but the narcissus is like the
      crocus both in its yellow color and its scent. Both flowers were sacred to
      Demeter and Persephone.

I am telling you the whole truth, though it grieves me."

So then all day with one mind
they comforted each other's heart and soul with many   435
embraces, and their spirits ceased from sorrow.
In delight they took joy from one another and gave it in return.
Then Hekate of the shining veil came near,
and many times embraced the daughter of holy Demeter;
from that time the lady Hekate became her attendant and
    companion.   440

And loud-thundering, far-seeing Zeus sent them a messenger,
fair-haired Rhea,° to lead dark-robed Demeter
among the tribes of the gods, and he promised to give her
whatever honors she might choose among the immortal gods,
and agreed° that the maiden would [spend]   445
the third part of the circling year beneath the misty gloom,
but two parts with her mother and the other immortals.

So he spoke and the goddess did not disobey the commands
    of Zeus.
Quickly she rushed down from the peaks of Olympos
and straightway came to Rharion,° a life-giving, fertile land   450
before, but then not fertile at all, instead it stood
idle, completely stripped of leaves. For the white barley
    was hidden
by the designs of fair-ankled Demeter. But afterwards
it was soon to grow tall with long ears of grain
as spring-time came. Then in the ground rich furrows   455
would be laden with wheat to be bound into sheaves.

There first she set foot from the barren upper air.
Gladly they saw each other and they rejoiced in their hearts,
and Rhea of the shining veil addressed her thus,
"Come here, child. Loud-thundering, far-seeing Zeus calls you   460
to come among the tribes of the gods, and he has promised
    to grant

---

442   The Titan Rhea was not normally a messenger goddess but, as the
       mother of Demeter and Zeus, would have been a logical choice to
       effect the final reconciliation between the two.

445   The verb in the Greek is "to nod"; Zeus' nod is the sign of his
       agreement and promise.

450   Rharion was a plain near Eleusis which was sacred to Demeter. Prizes
       of grain from this field are recorded for the Eleusinian games, and
       Pausanias (1.38.6) says cakes made from this grain were used in
       sacrifices there.

whatever honors you wish among the immortal gods.
And he has agreed that your daughter would [spend]
the third part of the circling year beneath the misty gloom,
but two parts with you and the other immortals.   465
He said it would be accomplished thus, and with his head
    he nodded assent.
But come, child, and obey me, and do not rage too much
without end at the dark-clouded son of Kronos.
But make the life-giving seed grow for men at once."

So she spoke and fair-wreathed Demeter did not disobey,   470
but at once made the seed rise up from the fertile soil.
All the wide earth was laden with leaves and flowers.°
Then, going to the kings who give laws,
she revealed to Triptolemos and Diokles, driver of horses,
and mighty Eumolpos and Keleos, leader of the people,   475
the performance of her sacred mysteries and taught her
    rites to all —
[to Triptolemos and Polyxeinos and, in addition to them,
    Diokles —]°
holy rites that are not to be transgressed, or asked about,
or discussed; for a great reverence for the gods restrains
    one's speech.
Blessed is he of men on earth who has seen these things,   480
but whoever is uninitiated in the mysteries, whoever has
    no part in them, never
has a share of the same joys when he is dead below the
    dank gloom.°

When indeed the shining goddess had taught them all these
    things,
the goddesses went to Olympos to join the gathering of
    the other gods.

470-472 In a later version of the myth Demeter grants the gift of agriculture
    to the Eleusinians in thanks for their hospitality to her and/or their
    help in finding Persephone. Here the return of her daughter leads her
    to restore crops to a people who already knew the art of agriculture.
    These distinctions reflect two separate traditions of the Demeter/
    Persephone myth, both of which may have been known to the poet.

477   This line probably does not belong in the text, since it repeats two of
    the kings already mentioned in 474. It may have been added as a gloss
    on "all" in 476, or could have belonged to a variant version.

482   The "joys" implied here are not specified, perhaps because they belong
    to the deeper Mysteries which are not to be divulged to non-initiates.

There they dwell beside Zeus, who delights in thunder,   485
holy and revered goddesses. Greatly blessed is he
of men on earth whom they love freely.
At once they send to his great house, by the hearth,
Ploutos,° who gives riches to mortal men.

But come, you who hold the land of fragrant Eleusis   490
and sea-girt Paros and rocky Antron,°
queenly Deo, giver of gifts, bringer of seasons,
you yourself and your daughter, beautiful Persephone,
in return for my song, kindly grant me heart-pleasing
        livelihood.
And I will remember you and another song.°   495

---

488   Ploutos ("Wealth") was the son of Demeter and Iasion (*Th.* 969ff.; cf.
       Od. 5.125-128). He is one of a group of deities known as the *theoi*
       ephestioi ("gods of the hearth") who were thought to bring good luck
       and prosperity to the house. Some scholars identify him with the
       unnamed divine child whose birth was announced as part of the
       mysteries at Eleusis, and as a god of agricultural prosperity, he was
       also later associated with the god Dionysos
491   The island of Paros (Map 1) was an important center of Demeter's cult,
       but Antron, in Thessaly (Map 2), is not connected with Demeter
       elsewhere.
495   This line is a regular formula for the end of a hymn. At 490-494 the
       singer calls directly on the goddesses, asks them to reward his
       devotion by granting him prosperity, and promises to remember them
       as he moves on to a new song.

3. HYMN TO APOLLO

Introduction

The *Homeric Hymn to Apollo* is one of the oldest hymns in the corpus, and the second longest after the *Hymn to Hermes*. According to the 3rd-century BC chronicler, Hippostratus, the hymn was composed by a man named Kynthaios from the island of Chios (Map 1), who "first recited the poems of Homer at Syracuse in the sixty-ninth Olympiad [= 504-501 BC]." If this evidence is true, the hymn must have been composed at least by 570 BC (given a generous estimate of Kynthaios' likely lifespan). But most scholars reject this date as too late, especially given the prominence in the poem of the Ionian assembly at Delos (see note on lines 146-164).

Another, related problem also confronts students of the *Hymn to Apollo*, namely whether it is one or two hymns. Lines 165-178 seem to bring to an end the first part of the hymn, which is devoted to praise of Apollo and his cult on Delos while the rest of the hymn is concerned with the worship of Apollo and the establishment of his oracle at Delphi (Pytho). This has led many scholars to suggest that the text we have now is a composite of two originally distinct hymns. One modern study of the language and diction of the hymn (Janko 1982) provides linguistic evidence that the two portions were composed by different poets at different times, and supports a date of ca. 690-640 BC for the Delian portion, and ca. 585 BC for the Pythian. Another study of the hymn's structure and content (Miller 1986) argues convincingly for the unity of the composition. Despite cogent arguments on both sides of the question, however, the poem's authorship and unity remain a matter of debate. My own suspicion is that the extant hymn is an intentional blend of two separate traditions which has kept the language of each (Delian and Pythian) distinct in many places, yet consciously structured the narrative to connect the most important themes and events of the two.

Whether or not the poem as we have it was originally composed by different authors, the narrative does represent a unified whole which celebrates two important events in the life of the god: his birth at Delos

(Map 1) and the establishment of his oracle at Delphi (Map 1). The opening of the hymn highlights the god's appearance on Olympos and the fearful reaction of the other gods to his presence. This scene, and the ensuing description of Leto's difficulty in finding a place to bear her son, points to a dangerous and violent side of the god which does not, in fact, appear except in the killing of the Pytho and punishing of Telphousa later in the poem. Before Delos agrees to be the birthplace of Apollo, she asks for a promise that the god will build a temple and an oracle on her land. Leto responds, promising a temple and honorific priority for the island, but no oracle (87-88). When the god is born, he announces to all present that his timai will include the bow, the lyre, and prophecy The end of the Delian section then describes the festival in honor of Apollo on Delos, including the songs performed by the Delian maidens. The narrative thus confirms the god's connection with the lyre, just as the opening lines proved his power with the bow. The final scene of joyous celebration likewise confirms the prediction of the delight to be brought to mortals by Apollo (25), in contrast to the potential of violence hinted at in the first scene on Olympos.

The "Pythian" section of the hymn picks up themes introduced in the Delian section and presents a narrative that is in many ways parallel to that of the first section. In a nice parallel to the end of the first section, the Pythian portion opens with a joyful scene of song, dance, and lyre-playing among the immortals on Olympos (186-206). Soon thereafter the poet moves to a catalogue of places Apollo visits on the Greek mainland in search of a site for his oracle. This catalogue balances that of the sites Leto visited before arriving at Delos. (Later in the poem Apollo completes another journey around the southern and western portions of the Peloponnese so that by the end of the hymn it is clear that his influence spans the whole Greek world.) Convinced by Telphousa not to found his temple on her site, Apollo goes instead to the slopes of Parnassos where he establishes his sanctuary. The narrative then details his slaying of the Pytho, a dragoness ravaging the area around his temple. Imbedded in the story of Pytho is a digression (305-355) on another monster, Typhaon, produced by Hera in defiance of Zeus after he dishonored her by producing a child, Athena, without her. Many scholars have considered this passage to be an interpolation added by a later poet, but the episode can be defended on several grounds. Among these, the passage provides a parallel for the potential threat Apollo himself might have offered to the divine order while at the same time echoing the picture of a hostile Hera offered in the beginning of the hymn. Apollo's slaying of the dragoness and his retribution against Telphousa for lying to him in spurning his oracle remind us that the god can be pitiless. With the oracle established, the remainder of the hymn details Apollo's last journey and kidnapping of Cretan sailors to become attendants at his sanctuary. Like the *Hymn to Aphrodite*, this hymn too ends rather abruptly with a warning to mortals to obey the god's will.

HYMN TO APOLLO

I will remember and not forget Apollo the far-shooter,°
at whose approach the gods throughout the house of Zeus tremble.
And they jump up as he comes near,°
all of them, from their seats, when he bends his splendid bow to
    string it,
but Leto° alone remains by Zeus who delights in thunder.   5
Then she unstrings his bow and closes the quiver,
and from his strong shoulders she takes the bow and quiver
in her hands and hangs them on a pillar of his father's house
from a golden peg; but him she leads to a seat and bids him sit.
And then his father gives him nectar° in a golden cup,   10
greeting his dear son with a toast, and then the other gods
take their seats there. And queenly Leto rejoices

---

1   Apollo is called "far-shooting" or the "worker-from-afar" because his customary weapon is the bow and arrows. The epithet is sometimes also used in place of his proper name. In this translation the term will be capitalized when this happens (e.g. 45).

3-13   In the original Greek, the poet shifts from the present tense in lines 2-4, to past tenses in 3-11, and back to the present in 12-13. This has led scholars to wonder whether the poet intended to describe Apollo's first entrance onto Olympos at some time in the past, or a timeless, typical entrance scene. I have used present tenses in the translation to stress the generic sense of the scene, since the fear Apollo can (and did) inspire with his bow is a central characteristic of the god and a clear sign of his power. It is important to recognize, however, that behind the generic lies the image of Apollo's first fearful appearance and the subsequent replacing of fear with joy at his entrance.
The fearful reaction to Apollo among the deities on Olympos is striking. On the "dark side" of this god, see 67n.

5   Leto, the first daughter of the Titans Koios and Phoebe (*Th.* 405-406), was the sixth mate of Zeus, to whom she bore Apollo and his twin sister Artemis (see genealogical chart); after this Zeus made Hera his seventh and "permanent" wife. Perhaps because Zeus sired so many children, the poets often identify them by their mothers.

10   Nectar was the drink of the gods. For their food, see 124n. below.

---

because she is the mother of a mighty son and archer.

Hail, blessed Leto, since you bore glorious children,°
lord Apollo and arrow-pouring° Artemis;   15
her on Ortygia,° but him on rocky Delos,
as you leaned against the great mass of the Kynthian° hill,
very near a date palm by the streams of Inopos.°

How then should I hymn you who are celebrated in all ways with
    many hymns?
For in every direction, Phoibos,° the field of song has been set out for
    you,   20

---

14   With the characteristic hymnic formula ("hail, god/goddess ...") the
      poet moves for the first time from narration of the topic at hand to a
      direct address to the deity. As he searches for the proper way to hymn
      Apollo, the hymnist will move back and forth between third person
      and second person narrative, e.g., addressing Apollo directly at 19,
      120, etc. The repeated direct addresses to the god (or goddess) by the
      poet, while not common in the other hymns (except in the ending
      formulae) is a characteristic feature of this hymn.

15   Artemis' common epithet suggests that she "showers" her target with
      arrows. While her brother's attribute is the bow itself, she is often
      shown just with a quiver of arrows. See figs. 2 and 3.

16   Ortygia means "Quail Island" and was, according to some, another
      name for Delos (Map 1), an island populated with quails. It was also
      sometimes called Asteria ("Star"), the same name Hesiod gives to
      Leto's sister who, according to Apollodorus, once transformed herself
      into a quail and threw herself into the sea, like a falling star, to escape
      the advances of Zeus. In this hymn Ortygia is distinguished from
      Delos, and may be the large island Rhenaia, west of Delos, as the
      ancient geographer Strabo thought (see Map 1). This is made likely by
      the inclusion of Rhenaia as the last place Leto travels to before
      reaching Delos (see line 44 below). Elsewhere (and later) the name
      Ortygia is also given to a small island in the bay of Syracuse. In spite
      of the tradition that Apollo and Artemis were twins, the author of this
      hymn was concerned only with the birth of Apollo. Pindar too places
      Artemis' birth on the separate island of Ortygia/Asteria which he calls
      "sister of Delos" (*N*. 1).

17   Kynthos is the name of the mountain on Delos where Leto actually
      gave birth. On the top of this mountain there was a shared cult to
      Zeus, Apollo, and Artemis, all of whom were called *Kynthios*. Among
      the Romans, Cynthia was another name for Diana (Artemis), who
      shared the same birthplace as Apollo.

18   Inopos was a small river which flowed at the base of Mt. Kynthos.

20   Phoibos is Apollo's most common epithet and is often used alone in
      place of his proper name. The word means "bright" and may refer to

both on the calf-nurturing mainland and throughout the islands.
All peaks please you and the high cliffs
of lofty mountains and the rivers flowing to the sea,
and the headlands which slope down to the sea, and the ocean
    harbors.

Should I sing how first Leto bore you to be a delight for mortals,°   25
as she leaned toward the Kynthian mountain on the rocky island,
on sea-girt Delos? And from either side a dark wave
rolled in towards the land accompanied by shrill-blowing winds.

Setting forth from there you are lord of all mortals:°
as many people as Crete holds within, and the district of Athens,   30
and the island of Aigina, and Euboia, famous for ships,
and Aigai, and Eiresiai, and Peparethos by the sea,
and Thracian Athos, and the high peaks of Pelion,
and Samothrace, and Ida's shady mountains,
and Skyros, and Phokaia, and the steep heights of Autokane,   35
and well-built Imbros, and misty Lemnos,
and holy Lesbos, the home of Makar,° son of Aiolos,
and Chios, which lies on the sea, brightest of the islands,
and rugged Mimas, and the high peaks of Korykos,
and bright Klaros, and the steep hill of Aisageë,   40

---

his connection with the sun. The same word in its feminine form
provides the name of his maternal grandmother, Phoebe.

25-139 After wondering how to begin his praise of Apollo, the poet settles on
the story of the god's birth on the island of Delos, which will take up
the first large section of the hymn. Because of this, the first part of the
hymn (1-176) is often called the "Delian" hymn to Apollo.

29   The next fourteen lines give a catalogue of sites where Apollo's cult was
actually established, but at the end (line 45) we learn that the list also
details the many places Leto visited in her effort to find a birthplace for
her son. This clever transition would surely have been more appreciated
by an ancient audience to whom the many place-names had more
meaning than they have for us.

The striking feature of this list is how great an area of the Aegean coast
and islands the sites span. See Map 1 for a majority of those that have
been identified with fair certainty. Both the number of sites and the wide
geographical area they cover attest to the importance of Apollo and his
cult, so the inclusion of the catalogue in a poem to him is appropriate.
As in other catalogues of this sort, the sites are not listed in precise
geographical order.

37   According to Homer, Makar was a legendary king of Lesbos (Il. 24.544),
but elsewhere he was said to be a son of Helios and from Rhodes. His
name ("Blessed," "Happy One") is a common epithet for the gods.

and well-watered Samos, and the sheer peaks of Mykale,
and Miletos, and Kos, the city of Meropian men,
and steep Knidos, and windy Karpathos,
and Naxos, and Paros, and rocky Rhenaia.

So many places did Leto approach in labor with the Far-shooter,   45
to see if any of the lands would be willing to make a home for her
    son.
But they trembled greatly and were afraid, and none dared
to receive Phoibos, even the more fertile ones,
until indeed queenly Leto came to Delos
and spoke winged words, asking her,°   50
"Delos, would you be willing to be the home of my son
Phoibos Apollo, and to establish a rich temple on your land?
But no one else will ever touch you, as you will see,
nor do I think you will be rich in cattle or sheep,
nor will you bear grain nor will you grow abundant crops.°   55
But if you have a temple of Apollo the far-shooter,
then all men will gather here and lead hecatombs,°
and the boundless savour of sacrificial fat
will always rise up, and you will feed those who dwell on you
from the hand of a foreigner,° since you do not have rich soil beneath
    your surface."   60

So she spoke. And Delos rejoiced and spoke in answer,

---

50   Delos here is considered both as an island and as a goddess or nymph.
       This personification of places was common in early Greek poetry and
       myth where rivers, mountains and cities were often identified with a
       minor local deity.
55   The island of Delos is small and has such rough and rocky ground that
       it would not have been good for farming or raising livestock, and thus
       not a good place to live.
57   A hecatomb was, at least originally, a sacrifice of one hundred oxen. In
       Ionia (Map 1) Apollo Hekatombaios was worshipped in a festival
       which gave its name to the entire month, *Hekatombaion*. Leto argues
       that the rocky island, whose barren soil cannot support crops or herds
       itself, will nonetheless become a desirable place for men to live
       because of the rich gifts brought by strangers to Apollo's shrine, and
       presumably the commerce these visitors will bring to the island. This
       prediction is accurate since, in fact, Delos was an important and
       central location for religious activity in the Aegean during antiquity.
60   The "foreigners" were those who came from other cities to worship
       Apollo. Since these worshippers would bring offerings (of animals,
       food, and other riches) to the temple, the priests living on the island

"Leto, most glorious daughter of great Koios,°
gladly would I receive your offspring, the lord
who shoots from afar, for it is terribly true that I am hateful
to men, and thus I would become much-honored.   65
But I tremble at this prophecy, Leto, nor will I hide it from you.
For they say that Apollo will be excessively violent,°
and will rule greatly among the immortals
and mortal men upon the grain-giving earth.
So I am terribly afraid in my heart and spirit   70
lest, when he first sees the light of the sun,
in scorn for my island, since I do have rocky ground,
he may overturn me with his feet and push me into the depths of the
      sea.°
There great wave after wave will wash over my head

---

	would be well fed even though the island itself was relatively barren. The same will be true for the priests at Delphi (531-539).
62	Koios was one of the twelve Titans born to Gaia (Earth) and Ouranos (Heaven) (*Th.* 133-137); see genealogical chart. Mated with another Titan, Phoebe, he has no separate mythology of his own beyond being the father of Leto.
67	The epithet here (*atasthalos*) indicates a kind of violence and reckless disregard for the consequences of one's actions which is probably akin to *hubris* (see 541n. below). It is a troubling epithet for a god, but is supported by the reactions both of the gods and goddesses on Olympos in lines 2-4 and of the other places visited by Leto (45-47), which suggest that Apollo did indeed have a dark side. His reputation as a god of great power and fierce anger dominates the hymn and can be seen elsewhere in Greek mythology as well. In the first book of the *Iliad* he brings a devastating plague upon the Greek army, in another myth, he mercilessly kills the children of Niobe with his sister, Artemis, and in another he is banished from Olympos for a time after killing the Cyclopes.
	Scholars have struggled to explain the negative view of Apollo suggested in the hymn. But it is characteristic for Greek gods to represent opposite poles at the same time. Thus Artemis is at once a huntress and the protector of animals, Hermes is a thief and a guardian of the house, Apollo is the god of healing, but also the god who brings the plague. In this light, it should not be so troubling to discover that the "most Greek" and most rational of the gods also has the potential for reckless and destructive actions. This potential (of which the islands and the other Olympians are aware and fearful) is never fully realized, but it is always in the background.
73	Even as a barren island Delos is at least able to support humans, and she now fears being turned into a reef fit only for seals and other sea creatures. We are probably not supposed to wonder how Apollo could overturn an island rooted firmly in the ocean. There was, however,

forever, and he will go to another land, whichever may please him, 75
to create a temple and woody groves.
But octopuses will make their lairs on me and sleek seals
their homes untroubled with no people near.
But if you would deign to swear me a great oath, goddess,
that he will build a very beautiful temple here first 80
to be an oracle for men, and then
[other temples. ...]°
among all men, since he will be worshipped under many names."

So she spoke, and Leto swore the great oath of the gods:
"Now let the earth know these things and the wide heaven above
and the flowing water of the Styx,° which is the greatest 85
and most awful oath among the blessed gods,
that in this place there will always be a fragrant
altar and sacred precinct for Phoibos and he will honor you above
    all."

But when she had sworn and finished her oath,
Delos rejoiced greatly at the birth of the far-shooting lord, 90
but for nine days and nine nights Leto was pierced
with labor pangs beyond hope. And the goddesses were within, all
who were the best, Dione,° and Rhea,

---

another ancient tradition (first recorded in Pindar) that Ortygia/
Asteria was a floating island which became anchored in place only
after the birth of Apollo. At that time it was named Delos ("Clear")
because, according to one interpretation, the island was no longer
invisible (*adêlos*) as it had been in the days when it floated free so that
sailors could not find it (cf. Callimachus *Hymn to Delos*). Our earliest
mention of a floating island is in Homer's description of the home of
Aiolos at the beginning of *Odyssey* 10.

81 There appears to be a break in the text ("lacuna") here, although it is
impossible to say if or how many lines are actually missing. An oracle
on Delos is attested by at least one ancient inscription, but it dates to
Hellenistic times. If the oracle existed for long, it apparently had
nothing like the importance or reputation of the god's oracle at Delphi.

85 The Styx ("the hated one") was a river in the Underworld and the
eldest daughter of the Titans Tethys and Okeanos; see genealogical
chart. In the *Theogony* (400) Hesiod tells how she received her role as
the most powerful oath of the gods, and what the processes of taking
this oath and paying the punishment for breaking it were (775-806).

93-94 Once again the poet delights his audience with a catalogue, this time
of the goddesses who attended Leto for the childbirth. **Dione** whose
name is the feminine form of Zeus, is, like Styx the daughter of Tethys
and Okeanos (*Th.* 353). She is also identified by some (including
Homer) as the mother of Aphrodite. **Rhea** is the wife of Kronos and

and Ichnaian Themis, and loud-groaning Amphitrite,
and the other immortals, except white-armed Hera,   95
for she was sitting in the halls of Zeus the cloud gatherer.
But Eileithyia alone had not learned of it, the goddess of childbirth.°
For she was sitting on the peak of Olympos under golden clouds
through the cunning of white-armed Hera, who held her back
out of jealousy, because fair-haired Leto was about   100
to bear a mighty and blameless son then.
But they° sent Iris° forth from the well-built island
to bring Eileithyia, promising a great necklace
fifteen feet long,° strung with golden threads.   104
And they urged her to call Eileithyia apart from white-armed Hera
lest afterwards with her words she turn Eileithyia back from going.
When swift Iris, with feet like the wind, heard this,
she went running and quickly covered all the distance between.
And when she reached steep Olympos, the home of the gods,

---

mother of Zeus and his siblings. **Themis,** also a Titan, is Zeus' second mate (*Th.* 901-906) whose name means "right, custom" and who, along with Gaia and Phoebe, was associated with the Delphic oracle by Aeschylus (*Eumenides* 1-8). For her role as nurse to Apollo see 124n. below. **Amphitrite** one of the fifty daughters of Nereus (and thus a sister of Thetis) was the wife of Poseidon (*Th.* 930). She is called "loud-groaning" (or "roaring") also at *Od.* 12.97, but whether the epithet refers to the sound of the ocean or to the sounds of a woman in labor is uncertain. According to other sources she attended the births of both Athena and Aphrodite. The goddesses in this catalogue are all of an older generation than the Olympians (see genealogical chart), and their antiquity lends importance to the event they will witness.

97   Eileithyia was one of the three children born to Hera and Zeus (the others were Hebe and Ares; see genealogical chart), and is the goddess of childbirth. She is important in Greek myth only when a birth is delayed by her absence, as at the birth of Herakles and here. The poet emphasizes the length of Leto's labor by mentioning her birth pains at several points in the narrative (45, 91-92) before Eileithyia's arrival brings about the final stage of the birth (115-119).

102a "They" are the goddesses mentioned in 92-95: Dione, Rhea, Themis, and Amphitrite.

102b Iris, a granddaughter of Okeanos, was the personification of the rainbow which stretched from sky to earth. She therefore was a messenger of the gods (cf. h. *Dem.* 314). Here she carries a message from the earth up to the heavens.

104   The Greek text specifies nine "cubits". A cubit was the distance between the tip of the middle finger to the elbow, roughly 17 to 22 inches.

at once she called Eileithyia forth from the halls   110
to the entrance and in winged words told her
everything, just as those who have their homes on Olympos° had bid
her.
And she persuaded the heart in her dear breast,
and they went by foot with the gait of timid doves.°

When Eileithyia goddess of birth-pangs, set foot on Delos,   115
then indeed did the final labor pains seize Leto and she longed to
give birth.
And she threw her two arms around a palm tree and pressed her
knees
on the soft meadow, and the earth below smiled.°
And out he leapt into the light, and all the goddesses cried out.°

Then the goddesses bathed you in bright water, noble Phoibos,°   120
with holy purity, and they swaddled you in a white cloth,
fine and newly woven, and they put a golden cord around it.
And indeed his mother did not nurse Apollo of the golden sword,°
but Themis poured drops of nectar and lovely ambrosia°

---

112   "Those who have their homes on Olympos" is a common epithet for the
       gods and goddesses. In this case it refers to Dione and the other
       goddesses who sent Iris to find Eileithyia (92-95).

114   This line is almost identical to *Il.* 5.778, which describes Hera and Athena
       walking with short, quick steps to join the best of the Greeks before a
       battle at Troy.

118   The smiling of the earth is a sign of fertility and the coming birth. Cf. h.
       Dem. 13-14 where the heaven, earth, and sea all smile at the blooming of
       flowers.

119   The description of Apollo leaping up at birth is very much like that of
       Hermes' birth (h. *H.* 20) and that of Pegasus and Chrysaor (*Th.* 281). In
       each case the newborn has extraordinary strength and divine power. The
       wail of goddesses is a ritual cry which marks the religious significance of
       the birth, as the smiling of the earth (118) signals the fertility of the scene.

120   Once again, the poet breaks his third person narrative to address Apollo
       directly. The derivation and meaning of his epithet (*hiē*) here are
       uncertain, but may be related to the Greek verb "shoot" and Apollo's role
       as an archer.

123   Why this Homeric epithet (*chrysaor*) is regularly applied to Apollo whose
       weapon was the bow, remains a mystery. It may refer to that god's battle
       with the Giants or with Tityos, since examples of ancient iconography
       depict Apollo with a sword in these scenes. Homeric scholia suggest the
       epithet may refer not to a sword, but to the strap on which his quiver or
       lyre hangs, or even to the rays of the sun.

124   In early epic poetry ambrosia was the food of the gods, as nectar was their
       drink. Some later authors (including Alcman and Sappho) reverse the

with her immortal hands. And Leto rejoiced   125
because she had borne a mighty son and archer.

But when indeed, Phoibos, you had gulped down this food of the
gods,
then the golden cords did not restrain you as you struggled,
nor did the bonds still hold you back, but all the ends were set free.°
And at once Phoibos Apollo spoke to the goddesses,   130
"The lyre and the curved bow are dear to me,
and I shall prophesy to men the unerring will of Zeus."°

So speaking Phoibos the long-haired shooter-from-afar
strode off on the widepathed earth. Then all the
goddesses were struck with wonder, and with gold all Delos   135
[was weighed down as she beheld the offspring of Zeus and Leto,
in joy because among the islands and the mainland the god had chosen her
to set up his home and held her more dear in his heart.]°
bloomed as when the peak of a mountain blooms with woodland
flowers.°

---

two. Both were thought to impart strength or immortality, and Demeter
thus anoints the baby Demophoön with them in h. *Dem.* 237.

That the goddess Themis ("Right") is the nurse of Apollo is no
coincidence, since the act of prophesying is closely connected with the
speaking of *themis* ("what is right") to mortals. When Apollo announces
at 252-253 and again at 292-293 that he will deliver prophecies to men,
the Greek verb used is *themisteuô*, and when the poet describes the
future role of the priests at Delphi they are said to announce *themistas*
("judgments"). For more on the importance of *themis* in this connection,
see 541n. below.

129   The theme of a god who cannot be held by bonds appears in the myths
of several other gods, including Dionysos (h. 7.11-15), and, perhaps,
Hermes (h. *H.* 409-413). In Apollo's case, the swaddling bands often
used to restrain the thrashing of a colicky baby, and thus to calm it, have
no effect at all on the young god.

131-132 Unlike his brother Hermes, who must steal his divine share (see h. *H.*),
Apollo simply declares that the bow, lyre, and prophecy will be in his
domain. The Hermes hymn accords the invention of the lyre to Hermes,
and gives a different explanation of how that instrument fell to Apollo's
lot.

136-138 These bracketed lines are probably a variant for line 139 and would
not have been sung along with it in a given performance. They appear
as part of the text in one manuscript and are added in the margins in
three others.

139   Although the scrubby land of Delos blooms not with real gold, but with
golden flowers, the effect is just as miraculous. The blooming of the land

And you yourself, lord of the silver bow, far-shooting Apollo,   140
sometimes walk on rocky Kynthos,
and sometimes wander among islands and men.
Many are your temples and woody groves
and all the peaks are dear to you and the high cliffs
of the lofty mountains, and the rivers flowing towards the sea.   145

But you, Phoibos, take the greatest delight in your heart for Delos,°
where Ionians with long flowing robes gather
together with their children and their revered wives.
And remembering you with boxing and dancing and song,
they delight you whenever they hold their contest.   150
Whoever came upon them when the Ionians were gathered
would say they were immortal and ageless forever.
For he would see the grace of all and would take pleasure in his heart
seeing the men and the women with their beautiful sashes,
and their swift ships, and many possessions.   155

In addition there is this great wonder, whose fame will never perish:
the Delian maidens, servants of the Far-shooter.
When they have first praised Apollo in a hymn,
and then Leto and Artemis who rains arrows,
remembering men and women of old   160
they sing a hymn, and they charm the races of men.

---

is another sign of the fertility associated with the birth. Cf. Il. 14.346-349
where the earth blooms with flowers when Zeus and Hera make love.
146-164 Thucydides (3.104) cites this passage in reporting the origins of the
festival on Delos; see General Introduction. At least by the 8th century
BC Ionians from the coast of Asia Minor (Map 1) and the islands of the
Aegean came to a yearly festival at Delos to honor the god, although by
the end of the 5th century a festival at Ephesos seems to have drawn
them away from Delos. This passage describes in detail the elements of
the festival, which was evidently open to women and children as well as
men and certainly included both musical and athletic contests. The
festival clearly drew participants from around the entire Aegean area,
and line 155 makes clear that these worshippers brought many riches to
the island (as Leto predicted at 56-60 of this hymn).
The passage concludes with a focus on the Delian maidens whose
description evokes that of the Muses themselves (just as the description
of the Ionians in 152 compared them to the immortals). These women
begin their songs with praise of Apollo, his mother, and sister (cf.
Hermes songs at h. H. 57-61, 427-32), but then move to epic poetry. In
these songs, the hymnist especially praises their ability to mimic the
different dialects of the festival participants.

And they know how to mimic the voices of all men
and their rattling of castanets. And each man would say that he himself
was speaking, so beautifully is their song put together.

But come, let Apollo be favorable° with Artemis, 165
and all you maidens, farewell. And hereafter
remember me whenever one of the earth-dwelling men,
a stranger who has suffered many trials, comes here and asks,
"Oh maidens, which man of the singers who come here
is the sweetest to you, and in whom do you delight the most?" 170
Then all of you answer about me:
"There is a blind man, and he lives on rugged Chios,
whose songs are all the best now and hereafter."°
And I will carry your fame over the earth as far as
I roam the well-inhabited cities of men, 175
and indeed they will believe it since it is true.
But I shall not stop hymning the far-shooter Apollo
of the silver bow whom fair-haired Leto bore.

Oh lord, you hold Lycia, and lovely Maeonia,°
and Miletos, the lovely city on the sea, 180
and you yourself are the great ruler of Delos, washed by the sea.

The son of glorious Leto playing on
the hollow lyre goes to rocky Pytho°

165-178 These lines seem to bring the hymn to a close, with the traditional plea
for favorable reception, and the farewell and promise to keep praising the
god. But the poet immediately launches into another part of the god's
story. Good arguments have been advanced on both sides for treating this
poem as one or two distinct songs, but the hymn as we have it is effective
as a whole. See introductory note.

172-173 Because the unquestioned master of Greek epic poetry was Homer,
these lines originated the ancient tradition that Homer was the blind poet
from Chios (Map 1) mentioned here. That Homer was in fact the author of
this hymn, however, cannot be true, and it is more likely that one of the
Chian singers (followers of Homer who called themselves the "sons of
Homer") composed this song and attributed it to the great master. For
more on the authorship of the hymn, see the introductory note.

179-180 Maeonia is a region of Asia Minor near Kyme and the Hermos river,
and Miletos is a city on the coast of Asia Minor, south of Samos (see
Map 1).

183 Pytho is another name for Delphi (Map 2). For the story of how Delphi
got this name (to commemorate the killing of a monster there) see 349-374
below. Because this second part of the hymn focuses on Pytho (Delphi)
and Apollo's establishment of a temple there, it is often called the

wearing divine, fragrant garments. And his lyre
has a lovely sound at the touch of the golden plectrum.   185
From there he goes to Olympos from earth, swift as thought,
to the house of Zeus to join the gathering of the other gods.
And at once the lyre and song are of interest to the immortals.
All the Muses° in unison answering with beautiful voice,
hymn the divine gifts of the gods and the sufferings   190
which men have from the immortal gods
as they live senseless and without resources, and they are not able
to find a cure for death and a defense against old age.
But the fair-haired Graces, and kindly Seasons,
and Harmonia,° and Hebe, and Aphrodite, the daughter of Zeus, 195
dance holding each other's arms by the wrist.
Among them sings one neither ugly nor short,
but very majestic to look at and impressive in form,
arrow-pouring Artemis, twin sister of Apollo.
And among them play Ares and sharp-eyed Argeiphontes.°   200
But Phoibos Apollo plays on the lyre
stepping high and beautifully, and around him shines a radiance
flashing from his feet and well-woven robe.
And golden-haired Leto and Zeus the deviser
rejoice in their great hearts as they watch   205
their dear son sporting among the immortal gods.°

How then should I hymn you who are celebrated in all ways with
many hymns?°
Should I sing of you among brides and in love,

"Pythian" hymn in contrast to the first "Delian" section.
189   The nine Muses, children of Zeus and Mnemosyne (Memory), were the
       patron goddesses of song and singers (*Th.* 52-63). See also h. *H.* 429-
       430n.
195   Harmonia was the daughter of Aphrodite and Ares, who married
       Kadmos, the legendary founder of Thebes (*Th.* 933-937), to whom she
       the bore Semele (the mother of Dionysos).
200   Argeiphontes is another name for Hermes. For more on the meaning of
       the epithet *argeiphontês*, see note on h. *H.* 73. The Greek verb (*paizô*) in
       this line (and in 206 where I have translated "sporting") can mean both
       to play and to dance. That Ares, the god of war, would be moved by
       Apollo's lyre to join in the dancing illustrates the power of the music as
       well as Apollo himself. For more on the power of music see h. *H.* 434n.
206   In this happy scene on Olympos there is no mention of Hera who, as
       Zeus legitimate wife, would normally be seated with him. The poet of
       the hymn has replaced her here with Leto to glorify Apollo the more by
       showing his parents sharing their pride in him.
207   This is the same line as at 19.

how you went wooing the daughter of Azan,
along with the godlike son of Elatos, Ischys, who has
    good horses?°   210
Or with Phorbas, born to Triops, or with Ereutheus?
Or with Leukippos and the wife of Leukippos —
the one on foot, but the other with his horses? To be sure he
    did not fall short of Triops.
Or should I sing how at first, seeking an oracle for men,
you went over the earth, far-shooting Apollo?   215

To Pieria° first you descended from Olympos,
and you went by sandy Lektos, and Ainianes,
and through the land of the Perrhaiboi. And soon you
    came to Iolkos,
and you stepped on Kenaion in Euboia, famed for ships.
And you stood on the Lelantine plain, but it did not
    please your heart   220
to create a temple and woody groves.

From there, crossing the Euripos, far-shooting Apollo,
you went up a sacred green mountain, and quickly you went
    from there
to Mykalessos and grassy Teumessos.
And you arrived at the seat of Thebes covered in forests.   225
For no one of mortals yet lived in sacred Thebes,
and there were no paths or roads at that time
throughout the wheat-bearing plain of Thebes, but woods
    covered it.
    From there, far-shooting Apollo, you went on,
and you came to Onchestos, to the splendid grove
    of Poseidon.°   230

210-213 The poet adds here another catalogue, this time of people rather than
        places. The daughter of Azan (elsewhere called the daughter of the
        Lapith Phlegyas) was probably Koronis, mother of Asklepios. Ischys, a
        son of Elatos, was Apollo's rival for her hand. Whether Phorbas and
        Ereutheus (211) were suitors of Koronis or other women is unclear.
        Leukippos (213) courted Daphne to no avail.
216   As the poet begins another catalogue of the places Apollo visited, he
        begins with Pieria, the first region the gods came to after descending
        from Olympos. It was also famous as the birthplace of the Muses. The
        travels of Apollo in this Pythian section of the hymn parallel those of
        Leto in the Delian portion. See Map 2 for a selection of sites on his
        itinerary. The "land of the Perrhaiboi" probably refers to the area
        between Mt. Olympos and Iolkos in Thessaly
230-238 Onchestos is located in Boiotia at the southern end of lake Kopais, to

There a new-broken colt, vexed as he is at drawing
the beautiful chariot, slows down to breathe, as its noble driver
leaps down from the chariot and goes his way; and the horses
for some time rattle the empty chariot, free from their master's
    control.
And if they should break the chariot in the wooded grove,   235
the men look after the horses, but tilt the chariot and leave it there.
For this was the rite from the very first. And the drivers pray to
the lord of the shrine, and the chariot falls to the lot of the god.

And from there, far-shooting Apollo, you went on.
Then you came upon the fair stream Kephissos,°   240
which pours its sweetly-flowing water from Lilaia.
Having crossed it, Worker-from-afar, and Okalea with its
    many towers,
then you came to grassy Haliartos.
And you made your way to Telphousa;° there the untroubled place
    pleased you
for building a temple and a woody grove.   245

You stood very near her and said,
"Telphousa, here indeed I intend to build a very beautiful temple,
an oracle for men, who will always bring

---

the north and west of Thebes (see Map 2). The rite described here, but
otherwise virtually unknown, is completely obscure and apparently
without significance for Apollo's story itself. It may have been included
here simply to please an audience familiar with the rite since the ancient
Greeks loved aetiolological stories about local cults and heroes.

The rite itself seems to have been performed as follows: In the grove
sacred to Poseidon drivers of chariots drawn by new-broken colts leap
from their cars and let the horses run loose. If the chariot is smashed, the
men take the horses but leave the chariot, propped up against a tree, as
part of the god's lot. The story sounds very much like the reenactment
of a perhaps long forgotten crash in the grove of Poseidon. The scene is
replayed to remember that god's power and to show him proper respect
by dedicating to him those chariots he chose not to protect.

240   Kephissos was a river which flowed from Lilaia, at the foot of Mt.
       Parnassos, into lake Kopais at its northern end. See Map 2. Okalea and
       Haliartos were northwest of Onchestos along the edge of the lake. The
       geography of this passage is unclear since, if Kephissos refers to the
       river, Apollo would not have crossed it as he travelled between
       Onchestos and Haliartos.

244   Telphousa is both a spring at the foot of Mt. Helikon and the nymph
       who lives in and oversees the spring. Thus Apollo can speak directly to
       her, as Leto did to Delos.

complete hecatombs to me here —
both those who live in the fertile Peloponnesos°   250
and those who who live in Europe° and throughout the sea-girt
    islands —
to consult the oracle. And to all these I would prophesy
unerring advice, delivering my oracles in the rich temple."

So speaking Phoibos Apollo laid out the foundations,
broad and very long from one end to the other.
    And when she saw it,   255
Telphousa was angered in her heart and said,
"Lord Phoibos, worker-from-afar, I shall put a word in your heart,
since you mean to build your beautiful temple here
to be an oracle for men, who will always bring
complete hecatombs to you here.   260
But I will speak out and you take it to heart.
The pounding of swift horses will always trouble you,
and mules drinking from my sacred springs.
Then men will want to marvel at
the well-made chariots and the pounding of the
    swift-footed horses   265
instead of at the great temple and the many possessions inside.
But if indeed you would listen to me at all — though you
    are stronger and
mightier than me, lord, and your strength is very great —
build in Krisa, beneath the fold of Parnassos.°
There no beautiful chariots will rattle nor will there
    be the sound   270
of swift-footed horses around your well-built altar.
But so to you as "Iepaieon"° they would bring gifts,
the famed tribes of men, and you, rejoicing in your heart,
would receive beautiful offerings from the men living around there."

---

250   The name Peloponnesos means literally the "island of Pelops" (*nêsos*
      Pelopos) and appears here for the first time in extant literature as a single
      word. It designates the southern part of mainland Greece (Map 2).
251   In Hesiod Europe is one of many water nymphs born to Tethys and
      Okeanos (*Th.* 357), but here (and in 291) the name seems to indicate
      that part of mainland Greece which is north of the Peloponnese.
      Pindar (N. 4.114) is the first to apply the name to the whole continent.
269   Krisa was the port of Delphi on the Gulf of Corinth, and Parnassos the
      mountain at Delphi. See Map 2.
272   This cult epithet combines the uncertain form *hië* ("shoot"?) with the
      god's early title as a healer, *paieon*, which can also refer to the song

So speaking she persuaded the mind of the Far-shooter, in order that
    she herself,   275
Telphousa, would have the glory in her land and not the Far-shooter.

And from there, far-shooting Apollo, you went on,
and you came to Phlegyes, the city of insolent men
who used to live on the earth with no regard for Zeus,
in a beautiful glen near the Kephissian lake.   280

From there quickly you went on toward the mountain ridge, rushing,
and you came to Krisa, beneath snowy Parnassos,
a foothill turned westward, but from above
a rock hangs over it, and a hollow, rugged glen
runs under it. There the lord Phoibos Apollo decided   285
to build his lovely temple, and he spoke a word:
"Here indeed I intend to build a beautiful temple°
to be an oracle for men who will always
bring complete hecatombs here for me —
both those who live in the fertile Peloponnesos   290
and those who live in Europe and throughout the sea-girt islands —
to consult the oracle. And to all these I would prophesy
unerring advice, delivering my oracles in the rich temple."

So speaking Phoibos Apollo laid out the foundations,
broad and very long from one end to the other. And on them   295
Trophonios and Agamedes, the sons of Erginos,°
dear to the immortal gods, set a stone threshold.
And countless tribes of men lived around the temple, to be a subject
    of song
forever because of its foundation stones.°

---

    worshippers sang in honor of the god (cf. 500, 517).

287-295 These lines are nearly identical to Apollo's speech to Telphousa at
    247-255, but this time the foundation of the temple is successful. There
    is no indication in the hymn that Apollo's temple was preceded by any
    other cult building, although other traditions point to a pre-existing
    oracle of either Gaia or Themis (e.g. A., *Eumenides* 1-20, E., *Iphigeneia at
    Tauris* 1234-1283). Either the hymnist did not know of these traditions,
    or chose not to mention them in order to increase his praise of Apollo
    as the founder rather than the usurper of the oracle.

296   Trophonios and Agamedes were architects also credited with a temple
    to Poseidon and several other buildings. Pausanias (10.5.13) records
    that the temple at Delphi which they were said to have built was
    destroyed by fire in 548 BC.

299   Perhaps troubled by the lack of detail about the temple's final
    construction, commentators have struggled with these lines in an

Nearby was a fair-flowing spring where°   300
the lord son of Zeus, with his mighty bow, killed a female serpent,°
a well-fed, great, fierce monster, which kept working
many evils against the men of the land, often against them
and often against their long-shanked sheep, since she was a blood-
    reeking bane.
And once from golden-throned Hera she received and nourished 305
Typhaon,° terrible and dreadful, a bane to mortals,
whom Hera once bore in anger at father Zeus,

---

attempt to force on the verb (*naiô* = "to live") the sense "to build," and to
explain or emend the epithet of "stones." But a complete description of
the building process is unnecessary since the remarkable aspect of the
temple was its foundation by the god himself. Moreover it is unlikely that
"countless tribes of men" would have been engaged in completing the
construction. Rather the poet seems to stress the ongoing importance of
the temple for generations of men and to refer neatly to his own hymn
when he says the foundation stones will be a subject of song forever.

300-374 The next 75 lines provide the story which will explain how Pytho got its
name, and Apollo his cult-title, after Apollo killed the unnamed serpent
which guarded the place. The narrative, however, is complicated by a
digression on another monster, Hera's male offspring Typhaon, which
takes up the bulk of the passage (305-355). In a ring composition typical of
the epic style, the poet moves from the encounter with Telphousa (244-
276), to a mention of the serpent which was menacing the countryside
(300-304), through the long digression on Typhaon (305-355), then back to
the point of the story, the threat she posed for men until her slaying at the
hands of Apollo (356-374), and finally ends with Telphousa's punishment
(375-387). That the Typhaon episode should be so carefully framed (as the
story of Odysseus' naming is framed by the description of his scar at *Od.*
19.392-466) indicates that it is particularly important.

Some translations use the term "dragon" for the monster Apollo killed,
but she was probably more like a serpent than our conception of a
medieval dragon. The killing of a serpent/dragon was a common theme
in Greek mythology. Best known, perhaps, are the stories of how Jason
killed the dragon which guarded the golden fleece (A.R. 4.123-182), and
how Kadmos slew a serpent before founding the city of Thebes (E.,
Phoenissae 657-931; Ovid *Met.* 3.1-130).

306   Typhaon is called Typhoeus at 367 below and in Hesiod. In the hymn
Typhaon is born to Hera in her anger at Zeus after the latter bears
Athena (see 309n. and 317n. below). In the *Theogony* (820-868) he is the
youngest son of Gaia (and Tartaros see genealogical chart), born in her
anger after Zeus' defeat of the Titans in their struggle for cosmic rule.
Hesiod describes him as a monster with a hundred snake heads which
breath fire and make sounds like those of many different animals. See
further in 355n. below.

because the son of Kronos had given birth to glorious Athena
from his head.° And queenly Hera was angered at once,
and she even spoke to the assembled immortals: 310
"Listen to me all you gods and goddesses,
how Zeus the cloud-gatherer begins to dishonor me
first, after he made me his devoted wife.
And now apart from me he has given birth to grey-eyed Athena,°
who is distinguished among all the blessed gods. 315
But he has grown to be a weak one among all the gods,
my child, Hephaistos, with his crooked legs, whom I bore myself.°
Taking him up in my hands I cast him and threw him into the wide
     sea.

309   Athena was born out of the head of Zeus and in some traditions was
      thus considered not to have had a mother. Hesiod tells the full story (*Th.*
      886-900) in which Zeus first mates with the goddess Metis
      ("Craftiness"), a daughter of Okeanos, and then learns from his
      grandparents (Gaia and Ouranos) that she is fated to bear a son who
      will become the king of gods and men in his place. To forestall this he
      swallows Metis when she is pregnant with her first child. Athena, the
      embodiment of her mother's wisdom, is thus born from Zeus' head,
      while he successfully incorporates Metis' qualities within himself and
      prevents her from bearing a son to overthrow him. See fig. 4.

314   Athena's standard epithet literally means "owl-eyed" but is
      traditionally interpreted as referring to the grey color of her eyes.

317   There are conflicting traditions about the birth of Hephaistos. In Homer
      he is the son of Zeus and Hera (*Od.* 8.312, accepted as such also in the
      Iliad by most readers; cf. 1.578), although three different stories are given
      about the cause of his lameness. According to one (*Il.* 1.590-594),
      Hephaistos says he was thrown down from Olympos to the island of
      Lemnos by Zeus for taking Hera's part in a quarrel against him.
      According to another (Il. 18.395-398) he claims to have been cast into the
      sea by Hera because he was already lame and to have been rescued
      there by the goddesses Thetis and Eurynome. In yet a third version (*Od.*
      8.311-312) he complains of being lame from birth and blames both his
      parents for the defect.
      Hesiod (*Th.* 927-929) preserves an entirely different version in which
      Hera gives birth to Hephaistos parthenogenically (without a male
      partner) after Zeus produces Athena from his head (without Hera's
      participation).
      The hymnist, who chooses the same motivation for Hera's
      parthenogenic birth of Typhaon, doesn't elaborate on Zeus' part in the
      birth of Hephaistos, but most readers assume Zeus is the father. Hera's
      anger in this passage clearly stems from the very recent appearance of
      Athena (314 "now"), whose birth was preceded by that of Hephaistos
      (316-321) who, in this version, has already been banished from Olympos
      and rescued again.

But the daughter of Nereus, silver-footed Thetis,°
received him and with her sisters she cared for him.   320
If only she had pleased the blessed gods some other way!
Shameful trickster, what else will you devise now?°
How did you dare give birth to grey-eyed Athena alone?
Couldn't I have borne her? And even so she would have been called
    yours°
among the immortals who hold the broad sky.   325
Take care, now, lest I devise some evil for you in the future.
And now, I shall contrive a way for there to be born
a child of mine, who will be distinguished among the immortal gods,
without shaming your sacred marriage bed or my own,
and I will not keep coming to your bed, but away from you,
far away, I will pass my time with the immortal gods."   330

So saying she went away from the gods, very angry.
Then at once ox-eyed queenly Hera prayed,
and with her hand turned downward she struck
    the earth and said,
"Hear me, now earth and wide heaven above,°

There may be a lacuna here since the Greek text has two main verbs without a conjunction in the relative clause, but if so, there is no indication how much of the story may be missing. This translation omits the second verb, *leipei* ("he/she leaves").

319   Thetis was a sea nymph and the best known of the fifty daughters of Doris (a daughter of Tethys and Okeanos) and Nereus, the "Old Man of the Sea," himself the son of Gaia and Pontos (Sea); see genealogical chart. Because Thetis was fated to bear a son greater than his father, Zeus refused to marry her and instead forced her to marry a mortal, Peleus. It was at their marriage that the goddess Eris (Strife) threw the golden ball inscribed "to the fairest" which led to the Judgment of Paris and the Trojan War. Thetis' most famous role is as the mother of Achilles.

322   An odd address to Zeus, except from Hera! Both the Greek verb *mêtiomai* ("to devise") and the epithet *poikilomêtis* ("trickster") preserve the same root as that in the name of Metis

324   The translation here assumes a slight change in the text (*ên ar'* for *êa r'*) now accepted by Càssola and Förstel. As transmitted, the text would mean "even so I was called yours...." The meaning here seems to be that the father gets the credit for the outstanding offspring (Athena), while the mother must accept the blame for the weak and deformed child (Hephaistos).

334-339 In this version of the story, Hera conceives and bears Typhaon for the same reason (and in the same way) she did Hephaistos in the *Theogony*, so that the two offspring seem to be multiforms of the same figure. From these lines, which also stress the role to be played by Gaia, Ouranos, and

and Titans, gods who dwell beneath the earth
around great Tartaros, from whom are descended
    both men and gods.   335
All these now hear me and grant me a child
apart from Zeus, in no way weaker in strength than he;
but let him be as much stronger as far-seeing Zeus is stronger than
    Kronos. "
So she spoke and struck the ground with her thick hand.°   340
And the life-bearing earth was moved, and seeing it she
rejoiced in her heart, for she thought it would be accomplished.

From this time on then for the full cycle of a year
she neither came to the bed of Zeus the contriver
nor did she keep suggesting shrewd plans as she had done before, 345
sitting beside him on her elaborate throne.
But staying in her temples where many pray,
ox-eyed queenly Hera enjoyed her offerings.
But when indeed the months and days were completed
in the course of the year, and the seasons came on,   350
she bore one resembling neither gods nor mortals,
Typhaon, terrible and dreadful, a bane to mortals.
At once ox-eyed queenly Hera took him
and then, adding evil to evil, she gave him up and the serpent took
    him.
He worked many evils against the glorious tribes of men.°   355

the Titans, it is clear that the monstrous offspring is intended to fulfill the role of the son who defeats the father in the cycle of succession myths familiar in Greek mythology. See further on 355 below.

340   Hera, like Penelope, is described as having "thick" hands. The epithet (*pachus*) plainly does not have the pejorative meaning that "thick hands" might suggest to a modern audience. One reader has suggested that it refers to the strength of a weaver's hand. If so, the use of the epithet would be complimentary since, for the ancient Greeks, skill at weaving was a virtue for women.

355   This digression on Typhaon/Typhoeus has seemed to some readers so far from the point of the hymn, that they have tried to expunge it from the text as an interpolation (a later addition by a different author). In fact, however, the story sets up a parallel which will become important for understanding the power of the god Apollo and the cult he establishes at Delphi.

Hesiod's Typhoeus is conceived by his mother Gaia in order to challenge Zeus for the ultimate kingship of gods and men, but is defeated and hurled into Tartaros (cf. also the later accounts of Apollodorus 1.6.3 and Nonnos D. 1-2.) In the context of the *Theogony* the story is clearly another step in the larger cycle of "succession"

Whoever met up with the serpent, his fated day carried him off
until the far-worker, lord Apollo, shot a strong arrow
at her. And she, racked with hard pains,
lay gasping great gasps, writhing on the ground.
And the awful sound was unspeakable, and through the forest   360
she twisted herself continually here and there, and she left her life-
          spirit,
breathing it out slaked with blood, but Phoibos Apollo boasted,
"Now rot here on the earth which feeds men,
at least you will no longer be an evil bane for living mortals,
who eat the fruit of the earth which nourishes many   365
and who will bring complete hecatombs here,
and neither Typhoeus nor accursed Chimera°
shall ward off a painful death for you, but right here
the dark earth and blazing Hyperion° will make you rot."
So he spoke exulting, and darkness covered both her eyes.   370
And on that spot the holy force of Helios made her rot away;
whence now it is called Pytho, and the people call
the lord "Pythian" eponymously because there

myths, characterized by the overthrow of each generation of gods by
the next generation (Ouranos—Kronos—Zeus), all with the help of a
female deity who takes up the side of the son (Gaia—Rhea—Gaia).
The potential threats to Zeus' power are handled with dispatch (his
refusal to marry Thetis, his swallowing of Metis, the war against the
Titans), and his defeat of Typhoeus ends the cycle for good and allows
him to establish a new order in the universe.

By spending so much time on Hera's anger and the subsequent birth of
Typhaon/Typhoeus, the hymnist fashions a strong parallel between Zeus'
defeat of that monster and Apollo's defeat of the serpent who nurtured
and raised Typhaon. The implication is clear that Apollo, like Zeus, will
now be able to establish a new order over which he will have ultimate
power, and that this order will be confirmed by the oracle at Delphi
whose foundation the hymn is celebrating.

367 According to Hesiod, Chimera was the daughter of Typhoeus and
     Echidna (*Th.* 306, 319-25); see genealogical chart. The name (spelled
     chimaira in Greek) means "she-goat," but the Chimera according to
     Hesiod's description had three heads, that of a lion, a goat, and a
     serpent. Homer, who tells of her death at the hands of Bellerophon
     (*Il.* 6.178-183), describes a monster who was "a lion in front, a snake
     behind, and a goat in the middle." In both traditions she breathed fire.

369 Hyperion was a Titan whose major role in Greek myth is as the father of
     Helios. In these lines (369 and 371) both names are used for the sun,
     whose heat causes the dead serpent to rot under its power.

on that spot the force of piercing Helios caused the monster to rot.°

And then Phoibos Apollo knew in his heart   375
why the fair-flowing spring had deceived him.°
And angered, he went to Telphousa and arrived at once
and stood very close to her and said to her,
"Telphousa, you were not after all meant to deceive my mind
by keeping this lovely place to pour forth your fair-flowing water.   380
Here too indeed will my glory exist, not yours alone."
He spoke and lord Apollo the far-worker pushed her against a cliff
with a shower of stones, and hid her waters,
and he made an altar in the woody grove
very near the fair-flowing spring. And there all men   385
pray to the lord by the name "Telphousios"
because he brought shame upon the waters of holy Telphousa.

And then indeed Phoibos Apollo considered in his heart
what men he should bring in to be priests,
who would be his attendants in rocky Pytho.°   390
As he pondered these things he saw on the wine-dark sea
a swift ship; on it were many noble men,

---

374   The story is given to explain the names of the place and its god from the
       Greek verb *pytho*, "to rot," in commemoration of Apollo's triumph over
       the monster on the future site of Delphi. "Pytho" thus means "the place
       where [the monster] rotted," and "Pythian" means "the one who caused
       [the monster] to rot." Given this context, it seems likely to me that
       Apollo was already associated with the sun by the time of this hymn (cf.
       also 440-445 below), although this point is disputed.

376   Telphousa has played the same role in this story that Gaia played in the
       Hesiodic account of Typhoeus' challenge to Zeus. After his mortal
       combat with the monster, Apollo realizes that Telphousa was not, in fact,
       sending him to a better, quieter place in which to found his temple, as
       she had indicated earlier (262-274), but rather sending him to a
       dangerous, threatening spot where his own future would be challenged.
       Her crime was not simply that of wanting to guard her own fame, but of
       wanting to subvert his. This is what causes his sudden anger and her
       final punishment (377-387) which concludes the story of the temple's
       foundation. (Why the god of prophecy was so easily duped in the first
       place is probably a question we are not supposed to worry about,
       although several rationalizations could be invented to explain it.)

390-544 The last section of the hymn explains the foundation of the cult at
       Delphi and why the god is called *delphinios*. Not mentioned at all is the
       central role which, in historical times, was played by the priestess of
       Apollo, called the Pythia. Either the hymn dates to a time before the
       Pythia acquired her position of importance in the cult, or the hymnist
       chose to suppress her in favor of highlighting the role played by the

Cretans from Minos' Knossos,° who perform sacrifices for the lord
and announce the judgments
of Phoibos Apollo of the golden sword, whatever he says   395
when he gives his oracles from the laurel beneath the vales of
    Parnassos.°
These men were sailing in their dark ship after business and profit
to sandy Pylos and the men of Pylos
going after business and profit. But Phoibos Apollo joined them.
Taking the form of a dolphin in the sea he leapt   400
onto the swift ship and lay there, a great and terrible monster.°
And whenever one of them thought in his heart to take notice of him,
the god would shake him in all directions and rattle the timbers
    of the ship.°
And they sat in silence in the ship afraid,
and they neither loosed the rigging along the dark, hollow ship,   405
nor loosened the sail of the dark-prowed ship.
But as they had set it up at first with ox-hide ropes,

---

priests. If the latter, it is possible that she was originally connected with the earlier Delphic cult of the pre-Olympian Gaia/Themis (see on 287-295 above). Her omission in this case would be in line with the priority given to the Olympians over earlier generations and to the male (Apollo, Zeus) over the female (Telephousa, the serpent, Hera) throughout the hymn.

393   Minos was the legendary king of Crete whose palace was located at Knossos. Why Apollo chooses Cretans to be his priests is not clear, but suggests that the hymnist believed in a close connection between Apollo's worship at Delphi and his cult at Knossos, where inscriptions indicate there was a temple of Apollo *Delphinios* (see further on 495 below). The Cretans in the hymn act as "Everymen," mortals no more distinguished than were the barren sites of Delos and Delphi which Apollo elevated to prominence. The present tenses ("who perform sacrifices ..") in lines 393-396 look ahead to the time when the hymn was composed and the oracle already established.

396   This line, especially in conjunction with the absence of the Pythia in the hymn, has led some to believe Apollo s original oracle was a tree-oracle like that at Dodona, where the priests interpreted the god's meaning from the rustling of leaves on a sacred oak tree. There is no good reason to accept this reasoning however. The role of the laurel in Apollo's cult is well established by other sources which tell us, among other details, that the first temple at Delphi was made of laurel, and that the Pythia chewed leaves of laurel before entering her prophetic trance.

401   Dolphins are not normally considered "monsters," but given the odd and threatening behavior of this creature, the term does not seem inappropriate!

402-403 It is not at all clear what these two lines really mean, but efforts to emend the text have been fruitless.

so they sailed. And a blustering south wind from behind stirred
the swift ship. First they went past Maleia,°
and by the Laconian land they came to a sea-crowned city   410
and the place of Helios who delights men,
Tainaron, where the deep-fleeced sheep of lord Helios
always graze and inhabit a delightful spot.
They wanted to put their ship in to shore there and disembark
to consider the great marvel and to see with their eyes   415
if the monster would remain on the deck of the hollow ship,
or leap back into the salty swell teeming with fish.
But the well-built ship did not obey the steering oars,
instead, keeping the fertile Peloponnesos on one side,
she went her way, and with his breath the far-worker lord Apollo 420
easily kept her straight. And traversing her path
she came to Arene, and lovely Argyphea,
and Thryon, ford of the Alpheios, and well-built Aipy,
and sandy Pylos and the men of Pylos;
and she went past Krounoi, and Chalkis, and past Dyme,   425
and past shining Elis, where the Epeians rule.
When she headed towards Pherai, delighting in the fair wind from
     Zeus,
then beneath the clouds the sheer mountain of Ithaka appeared,
and Doulichion, and Samê, and woody Zakynthos.

But when indeed she passed by the whole Peloponnesos   430
and, towards Krisa, the boundless gulf appeared
which closes off the rich Peloponnesos across its top,
there came a great clear west wind by decree of Zeus

409-437 See Map 2 for a partial itinerary of the ship. The sites mentioned are not
     given in geographical sequence, but generally trace a path around the
     south, west, and north sides of the Peloponnese beginning with Cape
     Maleia. Noteworthy too are the many echoes of Homeric language (429 =
     Od. 1.246, 9. 24, 16.123) and theme (the island of Helios, Ithaka) in these
     lines (and from here to the end of the poem). Several of the same places
     are also mentioned in the description of Telemakhos' journey home from
     Pylos to Ithaka at *Od.* 15.295-300. The apparently conscious allusion to the
     Odyssey throughout the final section of the hymn may have been intended
     to highlight the plight of the Cretans, removed from their ordinary world
     and, unlike Odysseus, forever denied a homecoming.
     Also worth noting is the care the poet takes to emphasize the role of Zeus
     in this enterprise (427, 433-435, 437). When Apollo finally reveals his
     identity to the sailors, he announces first that he is the son of Zeus (480).
     Apollo's authority and his glory are, of course, confirmed and enhanced
     by his position as the god who reveals the will of Zeus to others.

rushing boisterously from the sky, so that the ship
would very quickly make her way racing over the salt water of the
    sea.   435
Then back again toward the dawn and the sun
they sailed, and the lord Apollo, son of Zeus, led them.

And they came to shining Krisa rich in vines,
to the harbor, and the sea-faring ship touched the sands.
Then the far-worker lord Apollo leapt from the ship   440
like a star at midday. And from him many
sparks flew, and the blaze went into the sky.
And he entered° the inner sanctuary past the precious tripods.
There he kindled a flame showing his shafts,
and the light filled all Krisa. The wives   445
of the Krisians and the daughters with their beautiful sashes raised a
    ritual cry
at the force of Phoibos. For he instilled a great fear in each of them.
Then again swift as thought he made a flying leap onto the ship
looking like a man powerful and strong,
in the full bloom of youth, his hair covering his broad shoulders; 450
and he addressed them with winged words:
"Strangers who are you? From where do you sail the watery paths?
Is it on some business? Or do you wander idly
like pirates on the sea who roam about
hazarding their lives, carrying evil to foreign men?   455
Why are you sitting thus troubled, neither going out
onto the land nor stowing the tackle of your dark ship?
This is the custom of men who work for their bread,
whenever they come from the sea to land
in their dark ship, wearied by their toil, and at once   460
a desire for sweet food takes over their minds."
So he spoke and put courage in their hearts.

And the leader of the Cretans addressed him in answer.
"Stranger, since you are not at all like mortal men°

---

443   The verb here (*kataduo*) is also used of the sun setting — a nice touch if
      Apollo really was associated with the sun, as his description in 441-442
      suggests.

464-466 To address a stranger as though he or she were a god was not
      uncommon in early epic (cf. Odysseus to Nausikaä at *Od.* 6.149-169) and
      was a safe course to follow when divinities did in fact appear on earth
      (as here). See further in the note on h. *Aph.* 92-106 (where Anchises
      addresses Aphrodite). On the failure of humans to recognize gods, see h.
      Dem. 189n.

either in build or stature, but like the immortal gods,   465
hail and great joy, and may the gods grant you happiness.
Now tell me this truly so I may know it well;
What people are here? What land is this? What mortals are born
  here?
For intending otherwise, we were sailing over the great gulf
to Pylos from Crete, where we boast our race was born,   470
but now, not at all willing, we have arrived here with our ship
on another road, other paths, yearning for a return home.
But one of the immortals led us here against our will."

Answering them the far-worker Apollo said,
"Strangers, who used to live around Knossos with its many trees 475
before, now no longer will you return again
to your lovely city and beautiful homes, each of you,
to your dear wives, but here you will keep
my rich temple that is honored by many men.
I am the son of Zeus and I declare that I am Apollo.   480
I led you here over the great gulfs of the sea,
not intending anything evil, but here you will keep
my rich temple that is greatly honored by all men,°
and you will know the plans of the immortals, by whose will
you will always be honored continuously for all time.   485
But come, obey whatever I say quickly.
First loosen the ox-hide ropes and lower the sail,
then draw the swift ship up on the shore;
take your possessions and tackle from the straight ship,
and make an altar on the beach of the sea,   490
kindle a fire and offer white barley upon it.
Then indeed pray as you stand close around the altar.
Since I at first on the misty sea,
in the shape of a dolphin, leapt upon the swift ship,
so pray to me as "Delphinios;"° but the altar   495
itself will be "delphinian" and famous forever.

---

483   The repetition of lines 478-479 and 482-483 is perhaps meant for
      emphasis.
495   *Delphis* is the Greek word for dolphin and Apollo's cult-title *delphinios*
      will celebrate his miraculous appearance in the form of a dolphin on
      the Cretans' ship. Apollo Delphinios was the god who protected
      sailors, both merchants and colonists seeking new homes over the
      seas, and his cult is attested at several different sites. The poet hints at
      an etymological link between this title and the common name of the
      site as well, although nowhere in the hymn does the name Delphi
      actually appear.

Then make your meal by the swift dark ship,
and pour libations to the blessed gods who inhabit Olympos.
But when you have satisfied your desire for sweet food,
come with me and sing the paean°   500
until you come to the place where you will keep my rich temple."

So he spoke, and they listened closely to him and obeyed.
First they lowered the sail and loosed the ox-hide ropes,
and brought the mast down onto the mast-holder, lowering it with
    the forestays;
and they themselves set foot on the beach of the sea,   505
and they dragged the swift ship up from the sea onto the shore
high up on the sand, and they stretched long stays alongside it.
And they made an altar on the beach of the sea
and kindling fire and offering white barley upon it,
they prayed as he had ordered, standing close around the altar.   510
Then they took their meal beside the swift dark ship,
and poured libations to the blessed gods who inhabit Olympos.

But when they had satisfied their desire for food and drink,
they set off to go. And the son of Zeus, lord Apollo, led them
playing sweetly on the lyre held in his hands,   515
stepping high and beautifully. And beating time the Cretans
followed to Pytho and sang the paean
like the Cretan paean-singers and those in whose hearts
the divine Muse has put honey-sweet song.
Unwearied they came to the ridge on foot, and at once reached   520
Parnassos and the lovely place where he was destined
to live, honored by many men; and leading them
he showed them the holy inner sanctuary and rich temple.

But the spirit was stirred in their dear breasts,
and the leader of the Cretans addressed him asking,   525
"Lord, since indeed you have led us far from our dear ones and our
    fatherland
— for thus it was pleasing to your heart —

500 The paean (mentioned again at 517) was a song of rejoicing. At *Il.*
     1.472-474 it is sung by the Greeks to honor Apollo and again at 22.391-
     392 as a victory song after the death of Hektor. Paean was also the
     name of a Healer-god whose early existence on Crete is attested by the
     appearance of the name on a Linear B tablet. In later times Apollo was
     equated with Paean, since he too was a god of healing. In the
     following scene, Apollo leads his followers in the first paean which
     honors his own cult at Delphi (cf. Demeter's actions in establishing her
     worship at Eleusis, e.g. h. *Dem.* 192-210).

how shall we live now? Tell us this, we urge you.
This land is desirable neither for growing crops nor for pasture land,
so as to live well from it and at the same time to serve men."   530

Apollo, son of Zeus, smiled at them and said,°
"Foolish men, long-sufferers who desire cares
and painful toils and constraints in your heart,
I shall tell you a simple word and set it in your minds.
With a knife in your right hand let each of you,   535
slaughter sheep forever, and they will always be plentiful,
as many as the glorious tribes of men bring to me.
But keep watch over my temple, and receive the tribes of men
gathering here and especially [seeking] my direction° ....
If there is any idle word or deed,   540
and hubris° which is the custom of mortal men,

531-544 These lines comprise the first "prophecy" from Delphi as Apollo both answers the Cretans' question and warns them against treating their responsibilities at his temple too lightly. Because the land around Delphi is barren, the Cretans worry where their livelihood will come from. Apollo's answer makes clear that they, like the priests on Delos (51-60), will be fed from the hands of foreigners. In other words, their livelihood will depend on their faithful performance of the god's will. Scholars have tried to find in Apollo's prophecy of 540-544 a reference to particular historical events at Delphi (see introductory note to the hymn), but the warning can as easily be taken in more general terms: In spite of the riches which will eventually come to them and the power they will wield, the priests are to remember that they are servants of the god, charged with conveying *themistas* (cf. 124 above) to mortals. Only their ability to realize their own limitations in the performance of these duties will prevent them from putting their livelihood at risk. The sentiment here, as has been noted, is very much in harmony with the two famous maxims inscribed on the temple at Delphi in later times: "Know thyself," and "Nothing in excess."

540   There is probably a lacuna after this line, since otherwise there is no verb to go with "my direction."

541   *Hubris* is often translated "arrogant pride," but this is only a part of its definition. More importantly, the term commonly indicates the commission of acts which violate the norms set forth by a society (*themis*) and which are protected by the gods. Its range of meaning includes violence, moral transgressions, or even legal wrongs, and it generally involves insolence rooted in a sense of strength or superiority. *Hubris* leads man to disregard the gods and to act in ways which are offensive to them, whether by offering a direct challenge to a god's power (as when Arachne boasts her weaving is better than Athena's, Ovid *Met.* 6), or by overstepping a society's sense of "right" (*themis*) and thus offending the gods who uphold that value. The

other men will be your masters,
under whose compulsion you shall lie subdued for all your days.
All this has been told to you; you keep it in your minds."

And so farewell to you, son of Zeus and Leto, 545
but I shall remember you and another song also.°

---

suitors in the *Odyssey* provide a good example of this second kind of *hubris* in their violation of the accepted guest-host relationship, their excessive arrogance, and their increasing disregard for the gods themselves. The *hubris* against which Apollo cautions the Cretans is probably both the willful mismanagement of his oracle and, more generally, the customary tendency for mortals to believe too much in their own power (instead of Apollo's).

The importance of Apollo's warning is highlighted in the Greek text by the use of a charged word for "custom," *themis*. We have seen (124n.) that the root *themis* is used in references to Apollo's oracles, that the goddess Themis was the nurse of the infant Apollo, and that the term can refer in certain contexts to "what is morally right." So, although *themis* is used here primarily in its neutral sense as "custom," it also carries with it a host of other associations which are important in the hymn. To say that *hubris* (the violation of "what is morally right") is the *themis* ("custom") for mortals, sets up an interesting paradox which hints strongly that the Cretan priests will in the end fail in their attempt to follow Apollo's prophetic warning and be subdued by others. Historical evidence seems to confirm this since in later times Delphi claimed that its priests were *autochthonos* (native-born), not foreigners from Crete.

546 As in the other hymns, the poem ends with a regular formula, in which the singer bids his subject farewell and promises to remember him as he moves on to a new song.

4. HYMN TO HERMES

Introduction

The *Hymn to Hermes* is the longest poem in the corpus and almost certainly the latest of the long poems in composition. While there is no external evidence for the date or author of this poem, studies of the hymn's meter and language suggest a date near the end of the 6th century and an origin on the mainland of Greece, perhaps in Boiotia (Map 1).

The *Hymn to Hermes* differs from the other long Homeric hymns in its portrayal of the god as an infant and in the almost total absence of human characters in the narrative. Although the *Hymn to Apollo* recounts the birth of that god, he seems to grow to full stature almost at once and to conduct his affairs as an adult. While Apollo searches for a site on which to establish his temple in that hymn, there is no question about the domain which he governs, for he announces early on (131-132) his control over archery, prophecy and the lyre. In the *Hymn to Hermes*, on the other hand, the author plays with the image of the newly-born god from beginning to end, as he tells how this illegitimate child of Zeus, born relatively late in the cosmic scheme of things, works his way literally up from earth to the heavens as he defines the sphere of influence that will be his. The absence of humans in the poem, except for the old man of Onchestos, may be explained by the poet's wish to show Hermes' power not on earth, but among the Olympian gods, who have not yet granted him official entrance into their number as the myth begins. The hymn tells how this newborn god wins a position among the Olympians by challenging the status quo and, in the process, demonstrating the craft and cunning which will help define his official domain.

After opening with an account of Hermes' conception and birth in an Arcadian cave, the hymn details the god's activities over the next two days of his young life. The baby leaps up from his cradle almost at once, and sets off to steal the cattle of his older brother, Apollo. However, as he leaves the cave, he happens upon a mountain tortoise, which he greets and then kills, in order to use its shell to invent a new musical instrument, the lyre. After testing the new instrument with a song,

Hermes travels north to Pieria (Maps 1, 2) where he takes Apollo's cattle and drives them south again to the Alpheios river (Maps 1, 2), inventing sandals for himself and a trick for disguising the animals' prints as he goes. At the Alpheios he sacrifices two of the cows and, inventing a way to kindle fire in order to cook the meat, he prepares a ritual feast in honor of the twelve gods. Having completed the ritual without tasting any of the food himself, Hermes hides the remaining animals in a cave and returns to Kyllene to await the arrival of Apollo. The rest of the hymn deals with their confrontation and its resolution before Zeus and, finally, with the reconciliation of the two gods, brought about by Hermes' gift of the lyre to Apollo, and Hermes' acceptance among the Olympians.

Although the tone of the hymn is light-hearted and often humorous, the intent of the poem to honor the god is no different from that of the other hymns in the corpus. And, since Hermes is the trickster god of the Greek pantheon, this tone seems especially well-suited to its subject. But the craft of the poet in drawing on traditional themes and figures in composing the myth of Hermes' acceptance as a god has often gone unrecognized, and the hymn has been dismissed as inferior or ignored by readers in the past. A close look at the narrative, however, reveals intricacies worthy of Hermes himself. For our purposes, a few examples will suffice to illustrate the point.

Entwined in the myth of this god's rise to power are the traditional theme of the cattle-raid and the theme of the "first inventor". The hymnist uses these themes in order both to construct the narrative of the hymn and to effect the progress of the god within that narrative. So, for example, Hermes plans the raid on his brother's cattle, but stops to invent the lyre and music before finally stealing the cows. In terms of the god's purpose, it is the raid which will precipitate the crisis with Apollo, and the music which will resolve that crisis. So the hymnist, by way of a clever ring-composition, draws a conscious connection between these two apparently unrelated incidents, while at the same time preserving the picture of the new god as an innocent child moving from one activity to another, seemingly at random.

The language of the hymn in describing Hermes' theft of the cows, moreover, invites recollection of the Greek hero Herakles, known for his own raid on the cattle of Geryon and his miraculous exploits as a baby, but perhaps most of all, for his winning of acceptance on Olympos. Yet Hermes' raid is accomplished by stealth and trickery, rather than by the force usually associated with Herakles and other cattle-raiders. In this way, the hymnist draws on mythic traditions outside those of the story itself, while at the same time ensuring coherence of tone and characterization in the hymn. As Hermes defines the *timê* (honor, domain) that will be his by the end of the poem, the hymnist implicitly appropriates pieces of other myths in order to construct this new myth of Hermes.

In a similar way Hermes' sacrifice of the cows and preparation of the meal by the Alpheios recalls the story of Prometheus' unequal division of meat in the feast of gods and men at Mekone (Hes. *Th.* 536-549). While Prometheus' trick at Mekone resulted in a split between gods and men, however, the hymnist seems to portray Hermes in effect undoing the previous trick by taking care to make each portion equally honorable. Of course, the two feasts are quite different from the outset, and Hermes' actions in the hymn are calculated to honor the gods and show his own skill in the role of *kêrux* (herald), not to benefit mankind. So once again, the hymnist makes use of a traditional myth and mythic figure, not to draw a direct parallel with Prometheus, but to show the new god going beyond the traditional figure, making his own, new way, and thus crafting a new domain for himself among the Olympians.

By weaving together previously distinct themes and exploits from traditional myths, the hymnist provides a framework in which the newborn Hermes can establish himself as a cunning inventor and trickster, first by creating and then resolving a conflict with the god Apollo. In so doing, the young god proves himself worthy of divine status, and is given his own sphere of dominance (*timê*). This new domain, moreover, is one the god has carved out for himself through his actions in the hymn. So Hermes defines himself as a god who crosses boundaries of all kinds, a god with skill both in speech and at the feast (both skills central to his role as a *kêrux*), a god of thievery and exchange, a god associated with animals, music and minor forms of prophecy and, finally, a god of *mêtis*.

HYMN TO HERMES

Sing, Muse, of Hermes, son of Zeus and Maia,°
ruler of Kyllene° and Arkadia rich in flocks,
swift° messenger of the immortals, whom Maia bore,
the reverent nymph with the beautiful hair, mingling in love with
    Zeus.
But she avoided the company of the blessed gods,   5
living in a shady cave° where the son of Kronos°
used to mingle in love with the fair-haired nymph° in the dark of
    night,
unnoticed by both immortal gods and mortal men,
while sweet sleep held white-armed Hera°

---

1   Maia, a nymph whose name means "mother," is the daughter of Atlas
      (see genealogical chart), and appears in other myths only as the
      mother of Hermes (e.g. *Od.* 14.435, *Th.* 938).

2   Kyllene, a mountain in N.E. Arkadia (Map 2), is the most commonly
      accepted birthplace of Hermes and "Kyllenian" is one of his earliest
      and most frequently used epithets.

3   No one really knows the meaning of this epithet (*eriounios*), and some
      translations give "luck-bringing" or "crafty", but "swift" is the most likely.

6a   Like Kalypso (another daughter of Atlas) in the *Odyssey*, Maia chooses
      to live in a cave apart from other gods, and like that nymph her home,
      with its threshold (23), court-yard (26), and rich interior (60-61, 246-
      252) is clearly more like a house than a real cave. Nonetheless Hermes
      complains about having to live in a gloomy cave (172).

6b   Although Kronos had three sons, only Zeus receives the epithet
      "Kronios, " "son of Kronos. "

7   This is the same phrase used of Kalypso in the *Odyssey* (1.86, 5.30, 57-
      58) and continues the parallel between the two and their isolated
      dwelling-places.

9   Hera is both sister and wife of Zeus. In many myths she appears as a
      jealous wife, who remains angry at her husband and vindictive towards
      his many paramours and their offspring. This affair lasts an unusually
      long time for Zeus, and the hymnist seems to be having fun with the
      picture of him sneaking out of the house after his wife falls asleep.

But when the will of great Zeus was accomplished°   10
and the tenth moon° had already been fixed in heaven for her,
it° brought into the light a child and miraculous deeds were born.

And then she bore a child of many turns,° crafty of counsel,
a robber, a driver of cattle, a leader of dreams,°
a watcher at night,° a thief at the gates, who would quickly   15
reveal glorious deeds among the immortal gods.
Born at dawn, at mid-day he played the lyre,
in the evening he stole the cattle of far-shooting Apollo,°
on the fourth of the month° in which queenly Maia bore him.

---

10   Since the notion of Zeus' will being fulfilled is formulaic (*Il.* 1.5, *Th.* 1002, and *Cypria* fr. 1.7), we cannot be sure that it was Hermes specifically that Zeus planned to beget, but line 160 makes it likely.

11   The early Greeks divided the year into lunar months of 29-30 days each, so that the moon was equated with the month. The number of "ten moons" here also reflects their practice of counting inclusively. Thus Maia's pregnancy lasted roughly nine months (or 280-290 days). On different methods of reckoning time, see West (1978) 376-381.

12   The Greek text is ambiguous, but the subject of the sentence is probably the last month of the pregnancy itself which brings to light not only the child, but also the miraculous deeds associated with him.

13   This epithet (*polytropos*), meaning both "ingenious" and "much-wandering," is used elsewhere only of Odysseus, but fits Hermes' actions in the hymn especially well. Odysseus' maternal grandfather was Autolykos who, according to post-Homeric tradition was the son of Hermes. Homer mentions Autolykos' skill at thievery and notes he was a favorite of the god Hermes (*Od.* 19.395-398), but nowhere indicates a blood-relationship between the two. The epithet *polytropos* begins a list of seven consecutive epithets detailing Hermes' different virtues. This is a common feature in hymns and prayers which was taken to extreme lengths in later literature. Here, the epithets stress Hermes' crafty nature and ability as a trickster, characteristics well suited to the theme of the hymn.

14   The epithet reflects Hermes' ability to put people to sleep, as in the Argus myth, where this talent enabled him to kill the monster and free Io. The same power would, of course, ensure a thief of success.

15   Again, the epithet is double-edged since the "watcher at night" may be a guardian or a thief.

18   These two lines give a nice summary of the hymn's plot, which deals largely with Hermes' first 24 hours of life. The hymnist continues to mark events according to very specific times of day probably to highlight the speed and miraculous nature of Hermes' actions as he completes this first day (and night). Apollo is Hermes' older brother, but how and why the baby thinks to steal his cattle is not explained till later.

19   The Greek says literally "the earlier fourth" according to the ancient system which divided each month in half according to the waxing and

And after he leapt up° from the immortal limbs of Maia   20
he did not stay for long lying in his holy cradle,
but sprang up and sought the cattle of Apollo,
walking over the threshold of the high-vaulted cave.
There, finding a tortoise, he won endless joy.°
Hermes indeed was the first to make the tortoise a singer,°   25
as she met him at the courtyard gates,
feeding on the rich grass in front of the house,
going lightly on her feet.° And the swift son of Zeus
laughed watching her and immediately spoke a word:
"Already, a very useful token° for me! I do not scorn it.   30
Hail, comrade of the feast, lovely in shape, played at the dance,°

waning of the moon. Other methods of reckoning dates included counting 30 days in a month or dividing the month into thirds (with 10 days in each third). According to Hesiod (WD 770) the fourth was a holy day — and therefore lucky — but he doesn't explain why.

20   This is an odd verb to use for the birth of a baby, but it highlights Hermes' divine nature and extraordinary abilities. Apollo too springs forth from his mother (h. Ap. 119) as do Pegasus and his brother, Chrysaor (Th. 281).

24   In all other versions of this story (e.g. Apollodorus 3.10.2, Sophocles' Ichneutai, Eratosthenes' Kataterismoi 24), the tortoise episode comes after the theft of the cattle. The order here reminds us that Hermes is just a child, easily distracted by a new toy. As the episode progresses, however, we see Hermes' craftiness as he turns the tortoise into a lyre and invents a new kind of song. The music of the lyre will be important in reconciling Hermes and Apollo after the theft. See Introduction to this hymn.

25   A major focus of the hymn is the inventive power of the new god, and the hymnist stresses Hermes' role as an inventor, especially here and at 111. In the course of the god's first day and night he will accumulate no less than 10 "firsts," with at least another 4 occurring the next day.

27   The description of the tortoise prancing on her feet has bothered many readers since the epithet is used elsewhere of horses and dancing women. But the following lines (31, 38) make clear that Hermes immediately sees the animal in her transformed state as the sweet sounding lyre which will accompany dancers. Thus the poet's initially humorous phrase fits the tone of the hymn and the developing plot.

30   This word is significant since it signals the symbol by which Hermes will be recognized as a god. The hymnist plays with the connection between Hermes and the lyre by using the same epithet of each ("comrade of the feast" 31, 436) and by describing each in turn lying in Hermes' cradle (63-64, 150-152).

31-35 Hermes speech follows the model of the hymnic form (see General Introduction) with his initial greeting, a string of epithets which foreshadow the role of the animal in the poem, and his interest in the

a welcome sight! Whence did you, a tortoise living in the mountains,
clothe yourself in this beautiful plaything, this gleaming shell?
But I will take and carry you into the house, and you will profit me,
nor will I dishonor you; but first you will help me.   35
It is better to be at home, since the outdoors is harmful.°
For surely you will be a defense against baneful attacks
while alive,° but if you die, then you would sing very beautifully."

So he spoke and at the same time lifting her up in both hands
he went back into the house carrying the lovely plaything.   40
Then, after swinging her around,° he pierced through the life-force
of the mountain-tortoise with a knife of grey iron.
As when a swift thought passes through the breast
of a man whom frequent cares visit,
or when flashes whirl from the eyes,°   45
so glorious Hermes devised both word and deed at once.
And then, having cut stalks of reeds into lengths,° he fixed them in
     place

---

origin of the shell. His petition for the tortoise's help and
accompanying promise to honor her even mimic the standard ending
formula for hymns (e.g. h. *Dem.* 494-495, h. 6.20-21).

Lines 34-35 signal a kind of bargain between the god and the tortoise: by
giving up her life, the tortoise will gain endless honor as a musical
instrument. Ancient sacrifices regularly included a similar kind of
"game" in which the animal became a willing victim. In the Bouphonia
at Athens, for instance, barley would be sprinkled on the ground to
induce a cow to bow its head and thus "agree" to the slaughter.

36   This line is a proverb preserved also by Hesiod (*WD* 365).

38   The magical powers of the live tortoise are mentioned in several ancient
        sources, e.g., as a charm against hail. Pliny (*NH* 32.33) refers specifically
        to the powers of the dead animal's flesh and organs.

41   The meaning of the Greek verb here is not really known, but it seems to
        indicate the tossing of the animal in the air. Since the swinging of a
        tortoise (or lizard) on the end of a string was a game played by children
        in ancient Greece, the poet may have used this word to remind us that
        Hermes is a child as well as a powerful and clever god.

45   This seems to be the equivalent of our phrase "in the twinkling of an
        eye," to emphasize great speed.

47-51   These reeds will form either a bridge or tailpiece for the strings. At
        Archaic sites in Athens and Argos archaeologists have found pieces of
        tortoise shell pierced in precisely the way described here, but the exact
        function of the reeds remains unclear. The arms (50), made of goat horns
        and later of wood, fit into the openings in the shell for the front legs, and
        a wooden cross-bar linked the two near the top. Although one ancient
        tradition credits the seventh century poet Terpander with the invention

piercing the back of the tortoise through the shell.
And, using his wits, he stretched the hide of an ox around it
and he fit in arms and fastened the cross-bar to both,   50
and stretched seven harmonious strings of sheep gut to it.

But when he had finished, holding the lovely plaything
he tested it string by string with the plectrum,° and under his hand
it resounded awesomely. And the god sang beautifully to it
trying improvised songs, as when young men   55
revelling amid festivities trade mocking taunts.
Announcing his own famous birth, he sang
about Zeus, son of Kronos, and Maia, with her beautiful sandals,
how they used to converse in the companionship of love.
He honored both the handmaidens and the splendid home of the
    nymph   60
and the tripods in the house and the abundant cauldrons.°

So he sang of these things, but in his heart kept desiring others.
And, taking the hollow lyre, he put it
in his sacred cradle. Then longing for meat°
he sprang up from the fragrant chamber on the look-out,   65
in his heart pondering sheer trickery of the sort
thieves carry on in the hour of dark night.
Helios° was sinking below the earth into the ocean

---

of the seven-stringed lyre, our earliest illustrations make clear that this form was already known as early as 1550 BC. For illustrations and discussion of the different forms of the lyre, see M. Maas and J.M. Snyder, *Stringed Instruments of Ancient Greece* (New Haven and London 1989).

53   The plectrum, a straight or curved piece of wood, metal, or ivory, was like the modern guitar pick.

57-61 The song Hermes invents to go with the new instrument is none other than a *Hymn to Hermes*! This is an important indication of what the newborn god is really after, as his song looks forward to the acceptance into the Olympic pantheon which he is seeking. The description of Maia s cave in 60-61 differs radically from those he gives later and the handmaidens mentioned here do not appear elsewhere in the hymn.

64   The Greek phrase resembles that used of a lion ravenous for food (*Il.* 11.551 = 17.660). It is the first indication that Hermes wants something other than the nectar and ambrosia gods usually eat.

68   Like his father, the Titan Hyperion, Helios was a god of the sun. Each morning he drove his fiery chariot across the sky from east to west, and each evening travelled below the ocean back to the east. Homer never mentions the god's chariot, but it does appear elsewhere in the hymns (e.g. h. *Dem.* 63, 88-89). Later tradition identified Apollo as the sun god. Lines 68-70 stress the precise time the god arrived at his destination, just at sunset.

with his horses and chariot as Hermes,
running, arrived at the shady mountains of Pieria,°   70
where the immortal° cattle of the blessed gods had their pasture at
    night,
feeding on lovely unmown meadows.

Then the son of Maia, sharp-eyed Argeiphontes,°
cut off from the herd fifty loud-bellowing cattle.
He drove them on a devious path through a sandy place   75
turning their tracks aside. And he did not forget a crafty trick
making their hooves reversed°, the front in back
and the back in front, but he himself walked the opposite way.

And at once he wove sandals with wicker-work on the sandy shore,°
wondrous works, unimagined and unthought of,   80

70	Pieria, just north of Mt. Olympos in Thessaly, was the first region gods came to after descending from Olympos and was therefore a logical place for them to keep their cattle. In early literature and religion it was also famed as the birthplace of the Muses, who had a cult there. The distance Hermes had to cover from Kyllene to Pieria is huge (see Map 2).
71	The Greek adjective indicates divine ownership rather than strict immortality. These animals may, however, be like those of Helios which neither gave birth nor died on their own, but could be killed (Od. 12.130-131, 393). The parallels between Odysseus and Hermes in this hymn are strong, and there may be a connection between these cattle of Apollo and those of Helios (see 381-82n).
73	Although this is Hermes' most common epithet, often standing alone for the god's name as here, we cannot be sure what it actually means. Most likely is the traditional sense "Slayer of Argos," which refers to Hermes' conquest of the 100-eyed monster sent by Hera to guard Zeus' unfortunate girlfriend-turned-cow, Io (Ovid *Met.* 2.568-746). An alternate theory, "dog-slayer," is possible but could still refer to the same myth if the monster were a guard-dog.
77-78	Having diverted the cows onto the sand where their prints will be easily visible, Hermes marches them backwards but walks facing forward himself to confuse anyone who follows them. This trick is mentioned in Sophocles' version of the story (*Ichneutai* 118ff.) and in the Roman myth of Cacus (e.g. Vergil, *Aeneid* 8.210ff, *Livy* 1.7; Ovid, *Fasti* 1.550). In the Hesiodic version of our story (Ant. Lib 23), Hermes fastens brushwood to the animals' tails to sweep away their prints, and Apollodorus (3.10.2), perhaps conflating this part of the story with the invention of the sandals, has Hermes put shoes on the *cattle*.
79-84	These sandals are not to protect the newborn god's tender feet, as some have argued (probably based on his feigned excuse at 273), or he would not throw them away as he does before the end of his journey (139). The point is to leave further confusing tracks in the sand to dumbfound

mixing tamarisk and myrtle shoots.
Then binding together an armful of their fresh-budding wood
he tied the light sandals securely under his feet
with the leaves and all, which glorious Argeiphontes had plucked
from Pieria, as he skirted the path   85
like one hastening on a long road, in his own way.°

But an old man building up his flowering vineyard saw him
as he hurried toward the plain through grassy Onchestos.°
The son of glorious Maia spoke to him first.
"Old man with stooped shoulders digging around your plants,°   90
you will surely have much wine when all these bear fruit,
and yet although you have seen, do not see, and be deaf though
    you have heard,
and keep silent when what belongs to you suffers no harm."
Having said this much he urged the treasured° cattle on together.
And glorious Hermes drove them through many shady mountains 95
and blustery hollows and flowering plains.
And his dark ally, divine night, was ending, the greater part of it,
and soon the time just before dawn was coming to wake men to
    their work.

Shining Selene,° daughter of lord Pallas, Megamedes' son,

Apollo and illustrate once more his clever nature and quick mind. As
with the invention of the lyre, Hermes uses materials which are at hand,
so the tamarisk and myrtle mentioned here have no special importance.

85-86 The meaning of these lines is not entirely clear, but they seem to refer to
Hermes' unique method of travel: wearing new footwear he drives the
cattle backwards on a weaving course over the sand.

88   Onchestos, to the northwest of Thebes in Boiotia (Map 2), is known
chiefly for its grove sacred to Poseidon (e.g. *Il.* 2.506, h. *Ap.* 230).

90-93 There may be a lacuna after line 91 here. The old man is not necessary
to the plot of the hymn, but Hermes' warning for him to keep silent
about what he has seen recalls other versions of the myth where the god
turns to stone a witness who has been sworn to silence but who gives
information when the god returns in disguise to test him (Ant. Lib. 23;
Ovid, *Met.* 2.687-707). The description of the old man and his activities
here and at 188 is very like that of Laertes in the *Odyssey* (1.193, 24.224
ff). Although the sun was just setting as Hermes reached Pieria, and the
distance from there to Onchestos is large, there was still enough light to
permit gardening.

94   The meaning of this adjective is disputed. It refers either to the strength
or, more likely, the value of the animals.

99   In Hesiod (*Th.* 371) Selene is Helios' sister, daughter of Theia and
Hyperion; see genealogical chart. There Pallas, a son of the Titan Kreios

just at that moment reached her watch-post°   100
when the strong son of Zeus drove the wide-browed cattle
of Phoibos° Apollo to the Alpheios river.°
And they came untamed to a high-roofed cave
and water troughs in front of a bright meadow.
Next, when he had fed the loud-bellowing cattle well on fodder,   105
he drove them all together into the fold
chewing lotus and dewy galingale.

Then he collected many pieces of wood and gained the art of fire.
Taking a fine branch of laurel, he twirled it in a pomegranate bowl
fitted tightly in his palm, and the hot smoke flared up.°   110
Hermes indeed was the first to give us firesticks and fire.°
Then taking many dry, close-grained logs he put
an ample number in a sunken pit. And the flame shone

---

and Eurybia (*Th.* 375-376) and later husband of Styx (*Th.* 383), is Selene's
cousin. Since Pallas' brother sired the goddess Hekate (*Th.* 409-411) who
is also associated with the moon, his role as Selene's father here is not
without logic. In Roman tradition Pallas is the father of Aurora, goddess
of dawn. Megamedes is entirely unknown, but his name ("Great
Cunning") may be intended to link the night with Hermes' trickery.

100   The moon just reaches the tops of the mountains as she descends from
       the sky. Some editors have the moon rising here but if so it is rising near
       dawn since we have already seen that the night is nearly over (97-98).
       The poet uses four lines to stress that Hermes' trip to the Alpheios after
       passing through Onchestos has taken most of the night (and no wonder
       if he was driving the cattle backwards!).

102a   The epithet Phoibos, which means "bright," can stand with or without
       Apollo's name. As a sun god, his connection with brightness is self-
       evident, as is that of his grandmother, Phoebe.

102b   The Alpheios is the largest river in the Peloponnesos, flowing west of
       Olympia into the Adriatic Sea (see Maps 1, 2).

109-110 The meaning of these lines is disputed, with one manuscript reading
       in 109 "He took a fine stick of laurel and trimmed it with his knife ...."
       Most editors agree there must be a lacuna after this line since the
       process of kindling the fire would otherwise not be complete. This
       translation accepts a simple emendation of the reading in another
       manuscript which results in a description of the full process, well-
       known from other ancient sources: the laurel wood acts as a "drill"
       (held vertically) which bores into the wood of the pomegranate (called
       the "bowl" but perhaps simply another stick held horizontally) and
       creates fire through the resulting friction. This procedure is only a bit
       more effective than rubbing two sticks together.

111   As in line 25, the poet stresses Hermes' achievement as an inventor. The
       term "firesticks" is used here for the first time and refers to both pieces

afar sending forth a great blast of blazing fire.
But while the force of famed Hephaistos° kindled the fire,   115
meanwhile he dragged two bellowing cows with twisted horns
outside near the fire; for great strength came to him.
And he hurled both to the ground panting, on their backs;°
then he rolled them over, leaned on them and pierced their life spirits.
And he added deed to deed, cutting the meat rich with fat.   120
He pierced the meat with wooden spits and roasted
the flesh together with the prized back piece and the dark blood
contained in the intestines, and these lay there on the ground.
But he stretched the skins on a jagged rock,
so that they are still there now, long-lasting hereafter,   125
indeed long after these events and eternally.°

But then Hermes, rejoicing in his heart, dragged the rich cuts
onto a smooth, flat stone and divided them into twelve portions,
distributed by lot. And he added to each a perfect special portion of
    honor.°

---

of wood. Although Prometheus is credited by Hesiod (*Th.* 565-569, *WD*
50-52) and others with stealing fire for mankind, only Diodorus Siculus
(5.67.2) attributes the invention of fire (also from firesticks) to him. But the
consecutive scenes of fire and sacrifice here do recall the myth of
Prometheus who in many ways is a parallel figure to Hermes. The
hymnist exploits these parallels by using phrases and epithets from the
story of Prometheus throughout the hymn. See Introduction to this hymn.

115 "The force of Hephaistos" is another way of saying "fire" since
Hephaistos, as god of blacksmiths and forges, was so closely connected
with fire. This kind of expression is common in poetry, cf. Homer's use
of "Ares" to mean "death."

118-123 Hermes probably rolls the cows onto their sides for the fatal cut at the
neck. He then cuts up both animals and roasts those parts of the animal
which are edible. The chine, or back piece, was a choice cut, and the
intestinal sack of blood was considered a delicacy. This was the regular
procedure for preparing a meal with meat in ancient Greece, and while
the scene here is regularly referred to as a "sacrifice," we should
remember that whenever an animal was killed for food, a portion was set
aside for the gods. The focus in this scene is really on the meal.

125-126 The repetition in these lines is characteristic of the poet's style, but using
seven different expressions to say the skins stayed on the rocks sounds
even more awkward in English. That Hermes displayed the skins this
way shows he meant for his slaughter of the animals to be discovered
(and admired). This does in fact happen when Apollo sees them at 403-
406.

128-129 In sharp contrast to Prometheus' division of the meat at Mekone (*Th.*
536-549), Hermes prepares twelve even portions which he assigns by lot

Then glorious Hermes longed for the meats of the cult,° 130
for the sweet savour made him weary, even though he was a god.
But not even so was his bold heart persuaded
even though he longed very much to pass them down his holy
    throat.°
But he put them into the high-roofed cave,
the fat and many pieces of meat, and at once he raised them up in the
    air 135
as a sign of the recent theft.° Then, he piled up dry logs
and destroyed all the feet and heads with the fire's blast.

But when the god had completed everything as was fitting,
he threw his sandals into the deep-eddying Alpheios
and quenched the hot embers, and he levelled the dark soil° 140
through the rest of the night,° and Selene's fair light shone on him.

---

to ensure complete fairness. In addition, he adds to all twelve servings
a piece of the choicest cut which would normally have gone to only
one person at the meal (e.g. *Il.* 7.321, *Od.* 8.479-481). The text never
makes clear why there are *twelve* portions, but most readers agree that
Hermes is preparing a feast for the twelve Olympian gods, probably
already counting himself in their number.

130 Once again scholars do not agree on what the Greek really means here.
"Cult" in this case refers to a way of recognizing the honor or domain
(*timê*) of each recipient. In the cult of a god, ritual gifts and sacrifices
are a way to recognize the sphere of influence controlled by that god,
(e.g. Aphrodite over love). Hermes does not yet have a domain,
although his preparation of the feast, a function often performed by
the *kêrux* (herald) — points to his future role as *kêrux* of the gods.

131-133 No one can agree why Hermes refuses to eat the meat for which he
has been longing since line 64. If the food is intended to mark the *timê*
of the recipient, however, Hermes would naturally not yet be entitled
to a portion since his divine status has not yet been accepted by the
other gods. It is interesting that though he is a god, the smell of the
cooked meat weakens his resolve and tempts him greatly. His will-
power in this scene is like that of Odysseus in the *Odyssey* (especially
at 12.332 where he alone refuses to eat the cattle of the sun).

136 The text does not mention a shelf in the cave and, although the
description is a bit odd, it is likely that Hermes simply hung the meat
on the wall rather than miraculously levitating it into mid-air.

140 As he scatters the dust and embers, Hermes fills in the pit where he
first kindled fire (113).

141-143 Once again the hymnist takes several lines to stress the narrative's
time frame. The entire sacrifice feast episode and Hermes' trip back
home to Kyllene take place between the moment the moon descends
to the mountain-tops and the time dawn appears. With this "official"

And at once he reached again the shining peaks of Kyllene
at dawn, and no one met him on his long journey
neither of blessed gods nor mortal men,
nor did dogs bark. And Hermes, the swift son of Zeus,   145
turning sideways entered through the keyhole of the house,°
resembling a late summer breeze, like mist.
Pressing on he reached the rich inner chamber of the cave,
walking softly on his feet, for he did not make noise as one usually
    does on a floor.
Quickly then glorious Hermes went to his cradle.°   150
Wrapping his swaddling clothes around his shoulders like a young
child, his hands playing with the covering around his knees,
he lay, keeping the lovely tortoise-lyre close on his left.

But the god did not escape the notice of his mother, the goddess, and
she said,
"You rogue,° why are you coming back here and from where at this
    time of night,   155
clothed in shamelessness? I really believe you will
soon pass through the doorway with unbreakable bonds°
around your ribs at the hands of Leto's son,°
or you will be a thief, rushing here and there in the glens.
Go back! Your father conceived you as a great worry   160
for mortal men and immortal gods."°

---

    end of Hermes' first day, (since he was born at dawn the previous day,
    17), the poet stops emphasizing time so strongly in the rest of the hymn.

146   This is a nice, playful touch which could raise more questions than it
    would answer. Was Hermes locked out or trying to avoid the noise of
    opening the door? Was he just playing? Why did he have to turn
    sideways? The image certainly evokes the stealthy entrance of a thief (cf.
    159, 285). See also line 380.

150-153 Hermes' return to the cradle marks the end of his first set of exploits in
    a nice ring composition. The image of the god burying himself deep in
    his coverings recalls that of Odysseus covering himself in the leaves of
    the olive bush at the end of *Odyssey* 5 (487-491).

155   The Greek has an epithet here (*poikilomêtê* = "devious") which Homer
    uses exclusively of Odysseus. It is the same word Athena uses, both in
    fondness and exasperation, when she addresses Odysseus on Ithaka
    (*Od.* 13.293).

157   Maia anticipates here the very thing Apollo apparently tries to do to
    Hermes at 409 (see note).

158   Apollo, along with his twin sister Artemis, is the child of Leto and Zeus.
    He is often called "the son of Leto."

160-161 If this is true, Hermes' recent activities have certainly shown his
    fitness to assume such a role. Cf. 10n.

But Hermes answered her with crafty words,
"My mother, why do you aim these threats at me as if I were
a foolish young child, who knows very few evils in his heart
and cowers, fearful, at his mother's threats?   165
But I shall enter into whatever skill is best
to feed myself and you forever. And the two of us
alone among the immortal gods will not continue to stay here
in this place without offerings and without prayers, as you bid.°
Better to converse with the immortals all our days,   170
rich, wealthy, with much land for crops, than to sit
at home in a gloomy cave. And about honor,
I, too, will enter into the cult which Apollo has.°
And if my father will not grant this, I will try,
(and I have the power), to be a leader of thieves.°   175
And if the son of glorious Leto searches for me,
I think something else even greater will befall him.

167-169 Hermes worries that if he stays with his mother in Kyllene he will
        not be accepted as a full-fledged god among the Olympians. Equally
        important, unless he makes clear his status as a god, no humans will
        worship him. Hermes' complaint to Kalypso about the remoteness of
        her home at *Odyssey* 5.99-102 sounds very much like this. See 228-
        232n. below.
172-173 "Honor" here is again *timê*, the recognition of the god's power and
        domain, which is accomplished through ritual activities in cult. How
        the gods were each accorded their *timê* is a main topic of Hesiod's
        Theogony (112), and how a newly-born god receives *timê* is precisely
        the problem of this hymn (Apollo solved the same problem by
        announcing what his domain would be; h. *Ap.* 131-132). Hermes solves
        the problem in characteristic fashion by simply stealing the privileges
        of another god and using them to bargain for his own. Hermes makes
        his plan explicit here for the first time by announcing outright that he
        wants a cult equivalent to that of Apollo. He never explains why he
        has chosen Apollo, but the theme of strife between brothers is common
        in mythology, and Apollo's pastoral origin provides a domain (his
        herd) which is relatively accessible to Hermes. In addition, at 471
        Hermes credits Apollo with knowing the *timê* apportioned to each god
        by Zeus, so he may feel Apollo can be particularly useful in helping
        him to gain his own share. If so, this is confirmed first in 291-292 and
        finally at 516-517 when Apollo defines his younger brother's new *timê*.
175   Sounding very much like an angry child, Hermes follows Maia's
        threat at 159 with the retort that he wants to be a leader of thieves. In
        fact, this too turns out to be prophetic, since he has already shown his
        skill in this area and will become the god of thieves.

For I will go to Pytho° to break into his great house;
from there I will plunder splendid tripods in abundance and caul-
    drons
and gold, and gleaming iron in abundance   180
and much clothing.° And you will see it if you want."
So they spoke to each other with such words,
the son of aegis-bearing° Zeus and queenly Maia.

And dawn, the early-born, bringing light to mortals
was rising from the deep-flowing ocean. But Apollo   185
travelling, arrived at Onchestos, the lovely, holy grove
of the load-roaring Earthshaker.° There he found

178   Pytho is another name for Delphi where Apollo once killed a serpent
       and subsequently established his sanctuary and oracle. The *Homeric
       Hymn to Apollo* tells the full story, and explains the etymology of the
       name (from the Greek verb "to rot," 370-374) with an account of the
       serpent's corpse rotting in the sun.
179-181 From 60-61 and 249-251 we know that Maia's cave already has all
       these riches. The aim of Hermes' threat is not to gain material
       possessions but to prove his prowess as a thief and show his claim to
       divine recognition.
183   The aegis is usually understood to be a goat-skin (but see below),
       although it is described in a variety of ways in the Homeric poems. At
       Il. 5.738 and 18.203-204, for example, it is worn over the shoulders
       (figs. 5 and 6), but at *Il.* 15.307-310 Apollo is described as *holding* it, and
       Homer says that Hephaistos gave it to Zeus to frighten men
       (presumably by shaking it; cf. 15.229-230). One explanation equates the
       aegis with the *laiseion*, a complete animal skin worn by archers and
       held in front of them as a shield when needed (cf. depictions of
       Herakles wearing the skin of the Nemean Lion). The traditional view,
       supported by artistic representations, seems to have been that the
       aegis was, in fact, a shield covered by the fringed or shaggy skin of a
       goat (cf. *Il.* 2.447-449 where it is fringed with woven gold tassles), and
       whatever the original meaning of *aegis*, the early poets seem to have
       understood it this way.
       The derivation of *aegis* from the Greek word for goat (*aix*) is
       problematic, however, and there have been attempts to explain Zeus'
       traditional epithet *aigioxos* in a variety of ways. West (1978: 366-368)
       argues that the epithet is related to the words for goat (*aix*) and carry
       (*wechô*), and should mean "riding on a goat" or "drawn by a goat" (as
       Aphrodite's chariot was said to be drawn by doves). More recently
       Janko (1992: 230, 261) suggests the epithet may originally have meant
       "driver/holder of the thunderbolt" (with *aix* meaning "meteorite").
187   "Earthshaker" is another common name for Poseidon who, as god of
       the oceans surrounding the earth, was thought to "carry the earth"
       and thus be responsible for earthquakes.

a brutish old man building up the wall of his vineyard beside the
road.°
The son of glorious Leto addressed him first.
"Old man, berry-picker of grassy Onchestos,   190
I have come here from Pieria searching for cattle —
all cows, all with twisted horns —
from my herd. The dark bull was grazing alone
apart from the others, and the flashing-eyed dogs were following
     behind,
four of them, of one mind, like men. They were left behind,   195
the dogs and the bull, which was certainly an event of great wonder!
But the cows, just as the sun was setting, went
out of the soft meadow away from the sweet pasture.°
Tell me, old man born long ago, if by chance you saw
a man making his way after these cows."   200

Then the old man answered him and said,
"Friend, it is difficult to tell all that one sees
with the eyes. For many travellers journey this road,
some of these desiring many evil things, but others going back and
     forth
after the good, and it is difficult to know about each.   205
But all day long until the sun set
I was digging around the slope of my wine-producing vineyard,
and, sir, I thought — but I don't know for sure — that I saw a child.
The child, whoever he was, followed along with fine-horned cattle,
a young child, and he was holding a staff,° and walking from side to
     side,   210
and he drove them backwards but kept their heads facing him."

So spoke the old man. And, having heard his story, the other went
more quickly on his way.

188   Some translators read the line differently: "he found an old man
      grazing his brute (*knôdalon*), the stay of his vineyard, beside the road."
      This requires understanding an animal not mentioned in the earlier
      description of the old man (87-90). The current translation emends the
      verb from *nemonta* ("graze") to *demonta* ("build up") and takes
      knôdalon as an adjective describing the old man.
198   From this point on Apollo's story parallels that of the earlier narrative
      very closely and we are not meant to ask how he knew the cows
      disappeared at sunset.
210   The term (*rhabdos*), used for the staff which must be a walking stick
      here, usually refers to a staff (or wand) with magical powers, like those
      held in the *Odyssey* by Kirke (10.238, 293, etc), Athena (13.429, 16.172,
      45) and Hermes (5.47, 24.2). Cf. 529.

Then he noticed a long-winged bird and knew immediately°
that the thief was the son of Zeus Kronios.
Quickly the lord Apollo, son of Zeus, darted   215
to holy Pylos° looking for his shambling cattle,
his broad shoulders covered in a dark cloud.
And the Far-shooter saw the tracks and said,
"Oh! This is indeed a great wonder I see with my eyes!
These, at least, are the tracks of straight-horned cattle°   220
but they are turned back towards the meadow of asphodel.°
But these are not the steps of a man or a woman,
nor of grey wolves nor bears nor lions.
And I don't think it is any footprint of a shaggy-haired centaur —
whoever takes such huge strides with its swift feet.   225
They are strange on this side of the road, but even stranger on the
    other side."°

So saying, the lord Apollo, son of Zeus, rushed on
and came to the mountain of Kyllene, clothed in wood,
to the deep-shaded recess of rock where the divine
nymph brought forth the son of Zeus Kronios.   230
And a lovely scent spread throughout the sacred mountain,
and many long-shanked sheep were feeding on the grass.°

---

213   Whereas the function of the old man in other versions of the myth is to
      inform on Hermes, he does not do so here (see 90-93n). Instead Apollo
      learns his identity somehow by watching the flight of a bird. This was
      a common way for prophets to make their predictions and Apollo, as
      god of prophecy, speaks of this very art later in the hymn at 543-549.
216   This is not Nestor's Pylos in Messene (Map 1), but another Pylos
      located on the banks of the Alpheios near Olympia (Map 2).
220   Since the cattle are regularly described as having twisted or curved
      horns (116, 192, 567), it isn't clear why Apollo mentions the straight-
      horned kind here. Helios' cattle in the *Odyssey* (12.348) have straight
      horns and it is possible that the two traditions have become mixed in
      the poet's mind.
221   Elsewhere in early Greek epic "the meadow of asphodel" refers only
      to the Underworld.
222-226 After spotting the cattle's tracks, Apollo now notices the strange
      footprints left by Hermes' sandals (79-84) and cannot link them with
      any other known tracks. If the hymn really dates to the Archaic period,
      it is of interest to note that Archaic art represented the centaur with
      human front feet and horses' hooves in the back, a combination which
      would surely have left bizarre prints.
228-232 This description, like that of the cave's interior (248-510), again
      recalls Kalypso's cave at *Od.* 5.59-61, 68-71), and reminds us that the

Then, still rushing, the far-shooter Apollo himself
stepped down over the stone threshold into the gloomy cave.

And when the son of Zeus and Maia saw Apollo   235
the far-shooter furious about his cattle,
he sank down into his fragrant swaddling clothes; as when
wood-ash covers over the embers of tree trunks,
so Hermes rolled himself up when he saw the Worker-from-afar.°
And he drew his head and hands and feet together   240
like a freshly washed baby inviting sweet sleep,
though really he was wide awake. And he kept holding the tortoise-
    lyre under his arm.

But the son of Zeus and Leto knew and did not fail to recognize
both the beautiful mountain-nymph and her dear son,
a small child wrapped in crafty tricks.°   245
Then, having peered around throughout every nook of the great
    house,
he took a shining key and opened three cupboards
full of nectar and lovely ambrosia.
And much gold and silver lay within,
and many purple and white robes of the nymph,   250
the kind that the sacred homes of the blessed gods have inside.°
Then, when he had searched through the recesses of the great house,
the son of Leto addressed these words to glorious Hermes.
"Child who lies in the cradle, show me my cows
at once! Or else the two of us will soon quarrel outrageously. 255
For I will take and hurl you into gloomy Tartaros°

---

cost of remaining in this isolated paradise was the same for Hermes as
it was for Odysseus: the loss of his rightful domain and identity.

239   Apollo is called the Worker-from-afar, and sometimes the Far-darter,
because he is a god of archery who can shoot his arrows from a great
distance.

245   Hermes is, of course, physically wrapped in his swaddling clothes, but
the poet plays on that image by hinting that he is just as wrapped up
in his own plots. The word in the Greek, "twists," probably refers
obliquely to both. For Apollo and Maia standing over the swaddled
infant in the *liknon*, see fig. 7a and 7c.

248-251 These lines again make clear that Hermes already has plenty of
material goods. His challenge to Apollo is for a domain and *timê* of his
own.

256   Tartaros is the lowest part of the Underworld, into which Hesiod tells
us Zeus hurled both the monster Typhoeus (*Th.* 868) and the defeated
Titans (*Th.* 717-731), among others. According to the *Theogony* (720-

into dreadful and hopeless darkness. And neither your mother
nor your father will release you into the light, but below the earth
you will wander about, a leader among worthless° men."

But Hermes answered him with crafty words.   260
"Son of Leto, what is this harsh word you have spoken?
And have you come here looking for cattle of the field?
I haven't seen any, I haven't learned of any, I haven't heard any word
    from another.
I couldn't reveal them, nor could I win a reward.
And I'm not even like a mighty fellow, a driver of cattle;   265
this was not my deed, but up to now other things have been a con-
    cern for me.
Sleep has been my concern, and my mother's milk,
and having swaddling clothes around my shoulders, and warm
    baths.
Let no one find out about this, whence this quarrel arose.
And indeed it would be a great wonder among the immortals   270
for a child just born to pass through the doorway
with cattle of the field! Your story is absurd.
I was born yesterday and my feet are tender, and the ground below is
    rough.
But if you want, I will swear a great oath on my father's head:
I promise that I myself am not responsible   275
and that I have seen no other thief steal your cows,
whatever cows are; I only hear rumor of them."
So he spoke and, glancing shrewdly from his eyes,
he kept raising and lowering his eyebrows as he looked here and
    there,
with a long whistle as if listening to an idle tale.°   280

---

734) it lies as far below the earth's surface as the earth is below the sky, with Night wrapped three times around its neck and a fence with bronze doors surrounding it (cf. the description at *Il.* 8.13-16). The roots of Earth and Sea are above this prison but they, along with the roots of Chaos and Tartaros itself, have their source in the river Styx.

259   The sense of the Greek word (*oligos*, "little") in this context is open to debate, and has led to a wide variety of translations: "few men," "children," or even "the dead" (since souls are represented in art as miniature human figures). The thieves Hermes says he wishes to lead (175) would probably qualify among those worthless men "of little value", and Apollo's words at 292 make this interpretation all the more likely.

280   Hermes pretends Apollo's story is absurd, but looks sharply to gauge his brother's reaction.

Apollo, the worker-from-afar, laughed softly and said to him,
"Little one, you crafty-minded deceiver, the way you talk I do believe
you have broken into well-built houses many times
in the night and have made not just one man sit on the threshold,°
by ransacking through his house without a sound.   285
And you will grieve many shepherds dwelling in the fields
in mountain glens, whenever, craving meat,
you come upon their herds of cattle and their woolly sheep.
But come, lest you sleep for the last and final time,
come down from your cradle, you companion of dark night.   290
For from now on you will have this honor among the immortals:
you will be called a leader of thieves forever."°

So he spoke and, taking the child, Phoibos Apollo began to carry him.
But then indeed the powerful Argeiphontes, making a plan
as he was raised in Apollo's hands, sent forth an omen,   295
a stout worker of the belly, a wretched messenger.
And quickly after it he sneezed, and Apollo heard it,
and threw glorious Hermes to the ground from his hands.°
And even though he was eager for his journey, he sat before him
mocking Hermes, and he spoke a word to him.   300
"Never fear, swaddled son of Zeus and Maia.
in the end I will find the costly head of cattle
by these omens, and you will lead the way yet."°

So he spoke, and Kyllenian Hermes quickly sprang up in turn
moving in earnest. And with his hands he pushed the swaddling-
        cloth   305
around his shoulders, up over his ears, huddling himself together,°

---

284   This odd phrase may mean to indicate that the house is stripped of all
       its furniture, leaving no chairs on which to sit, or that the victim has
       been so thoroughly defeated that he sinks to the floor in despair.
       Interpreted another way, it could mean Hermes forces men to sit at
       guard on their thresholds as he tries to break in to their houses.

291-292 This is the first step in Hermes' acquisition of his own *timê* and a
       confirmation of his skill in stealing the cattle.

295-298 Hermes here noisily passes gas, although it is impossible to tell
       which end of his anatomy emits the omen, but in either case it is easy
       to see why Apollo does not want to hold this unpredictable baby too
       close. A sneeze is a common omen which may be favorable or
       unfavorable depending on the circumstances, but the older god is
       clearly taking no chances!

303   There is a nice irony in this threat since it also foreshadows Hermes'
       future role as a guide. See 392n. below.

306   These lines, which show Hermes in his disarming pose as a sleepy

and said,
"Where are you carrying me, Far-shooter, most violent of all the gods?
Are you provoking me in anger because of your cows?
—Oh, if only the herd of cattle would perish! For I did not
steal your cows, nor did I see another do it,   310
whatever cows are; I still only hear rumor of them.
Submit to and receive arbitration before Zeus Kronios."

But after Hermes the shepherd and the glorious son of Leto
questioned each other explicitly on each point,
being angry on both sides, the latter speaking the truth°   315
. . . .
Not unjustly did he try to grab Hermes on account of the cattle,
but the Kyllenian wanted to deceive the Lord of the Silver Bow
with crafty tricks and cunning words.
But when, although he was very crafty, he found Apollo with many
    resources,
then indeed he went forward quickly over the sand,   320
but the son of Zeus and Leto went behind.

And the splendid children of Zeus came at once to the summit
of fragrant Olympos to their father Kronios.
For there the justice-talents were set down by each.°
And a calm held snowy Olympos, but the deathless   325
immortals were beginning to gather after golden-throned dawn.
Both Hermes and Apollo of the silver bow stood
before the knees of Zeus, and high-thundering Zeus
questioned his shining son and spoke to him.

---

baby, at the same time contain a verb which in Homer often describes a
hero crouching to gather strength before an attack.

315 After this line there is a break in the text of uncertain length, signalled in
the translation by a line of dashes.

324 The Greek word for "talent" can mean either a measure of gold (silver,
etc.) or, when plural, the scales in which Zeus weighs the fates of
mortals in the *Iliad* (e.g. 8.69, 16.658). Most translations for this line
choose "scales of justice" which is, however, a Hellenistic notion
(though the 5th-century poet Bacchylides does speak of a "scale" of
justice; 17.25-26). Since Zeus does not use his scales to judge between
gods in the *Iliad*, and since no mention of them is made later in the
hymn, this translation is based on the other (and more common)
meaning of the word. Achilles' shield (*Il.* 18.497-508) shows a scene of
arbitration in which each litigant apparently deposits one talent for the
judge who gave the fairest judgment. This line in the hymn may be
meant to indicate a similar place of justice, although neither Apollo nor
Hermes is actually described as following this procedure.

"Phoibos, from where do you drive this plentiful booty,   330
this newly born child who has the look of a herald?°
This is a serious matter that has come before the assembly of the
    gods."

Then the lord Apollo who works from afar spoke to him,
"Father, soon you will hear no empty tale,
though you mock me for being the only one fond of gain.   335
In the mountains of Kyllene after a long journey,
I found a child, this piercing ravager here,
scornful, such as no other I have seen of gods
or men, as many as are thieves upon the earth.
And, having stolen my cows from the meadow, he went   340
along the shore of the load-roaring sea driving them at evening,
and drove them straight to Pylos. And there were two kinds of tracks,
    wondrous,
the sort to marvel at and the work of an illustrious god.
For, in the case of the cows, the black dust revealed
hoofprints reversed towards the flowery meadow,   345
but this one himself, shifty, unmanageable, went over
the sandy ground neither on his feet nor on his hands;
but using some other craft he wore such wondrous
ruts, as if someone were walking on slender oak trees.
So, as long as he was hurrying over the sandy place,   350
all the tracks were very easy to see in the dust.
But when he passed through the great path of the sand,
the cows' tracks and his own quickly became undiscernible
on the hard ground. But a mortal man noticed him
driving the race of wide-browed cows straight to Pylos.   355
But when indeed he had shut them up quietly
and worked his trickery here and there on the road,°
he lay down in his cradle like dark night
in the gloom of his dim cave; and not even
a sharp-eyed eagle could have seen him. But he rubbed   360
his eyes a lot with his hands, as he took care for his trickery.
Then at once he himself spoke without restraint,
'I haven't seen any, I haven't learned of any, I haven't heard any
    word from another.

331   Just as Hermes at once saw the tortoise in her future role as a "companion
      of the feast," now Zeus already sees Hermes as the herald of the gods.
357   This verb is an emendation for the otherwise nonsensical reading in the
      text. It refers to Hermes' craft in making the strange sandal prints on each
      side of the road.

I couldn't reveal them, nor could I win a reward.' "
Then, after saying these things, Phoibos Apollo sat down.   365

But Hermes told another story among the immortals
and explained to Kronios, leader of all the gods,
"Father Zeus, indeed I will tell you the truth,
for I am truthful and do not know how to lie.
He came to our house searching for his shambling cattle   370
today just as the sun was rising,
and he brought no witness and no overseer from the immortal gods.°
And he ordered me with much force to reveal them
and many times he threatened to hurl me into broad Tartaros
because he has the fresh bloom of glory-loving youth.   375
But I was born yesterday. And even he himself knows this,
that I am not at all like a mighty fellow, a driver of cattle.
Believe me — for you declare that you are my father° —
that I did not drive his cattle to my home (so may I prosper),
and I did not go over the threshold.° And I am saying
       this precisely.   380
But I greatly revere Helios° and the other gods,
and I love you and am in awe of this one. And you yourself know
that I am not responsible. But I take a great oath;
No! by these well-adorned doorways of the immortals.
And at another time I will repay him for his pitiless search   385
even though he is stronger. But you, defend the younger one!"
So spoke Kyllenian Argeiphontes, winking,
and he kept holding the swaddling cloth on his arm and did not cast
       it off.°

---

372   This seems to be early evidence for a kind of "due process" to be
      followed in making searches before a legal case.
378   Hermes boldly reverses the regular Homeric formula in which a man
      boasts that he is someone's son. Polyphemos does the same when he
      wants justice from his father, Poseidon at *Od.* 9.529.
380   Strictly speaking, this part of his story is true (cf. 146), but most of
      Hermes' denials are outright lies.
381   Helios here may be Apollo, although the earliest certain identification
      of the two doesn't occur elsewhere until Aeschylus (cf. h. *Ap.* 374n).
      Some readers have seen this mention of Helios as an attempt to disarm
      a witness since, as the sun who proverbially sees all things (cf. h. *Dem.*
      26), he was often called on in oaths. But since Hermes' theft of the
      cattle took place at night, this seems unlikely.
387-388 It isn't clear whether Hermes is hinting at his deception by winking
      (which Zeus' reaction at 389-391 suggests is likely), or whether he is

Zeus laughed loudly when he saw his mischievous son
making denials so well and skilfully about the cattle.   390
But he ordered both in common spirit
to search for the cattle, and Hermes the guide° to lead the way,
and, without planning harm, to show the place
where he had hidden the treasured heads of cattle.
Then the son of Kronos nodded and glorious Hermes obeyed,   395
for the will of aegis-bearing Zeus easily persuaded him.

And the two splendid children of Zeus hastened
to sandy Pylos, and came to the ford of the Alpheios.
And they reached the fields and the high-roofed cave
where Apollo's property had been tended in the dark of the night. 400
Then Hermes going into the rocky cave
drove the strong treasured heads of cattle out into the light.
But the son of Leto, looking to one side, noticed the cow-hides
on the steep rock, and quickly began to question glorious Hermes.
"How were you able to slit the throats of two cows, you crafty
    schemer,   405
though you are so newly born and weak? I myself
marvel at the power you will have in the future. There is no need at
    all
for you to grow large, Kyllenian son of Maia."
So he spoke, and with his hands he twisted strong bonds°
of willow, but these at once grew down into the ground beneath their

"blinking" as a sleepy baby would do. In either case, he keeps the
swaddling cloth around him both to preserve his image as an innocent
babe and, at the same time, to conceal the lyre which he has brought
with him.

392   Although *diaktoros* is a common epithet of the god in early epic, its
precise meaning is unknown. If "guide" is right, the poet's use of it in
this context is a nice touch since Hermes would be performing this
function for the first time here. In any case his actions here prove
Apollo's forecast at 303 entirely correct.

409   There may be a lacuna after this line since the existing text does not
explain who and what the bonds were for. Most likely Apollo tries to tie
Hermes, who shows his power again by making the willows root to the
ground and envelop the cattle instead. It is a characteristic of powerful
gods that bonds usually can not hold them (especially Dionysos e.g. at
h. 7.11-15 and Euripides *Bacchae* 436-450, 498, 616-17). Zeus' chaining of
Hera at *Il.* 15.18-22, and Hephaistos' binding of Ares and Aphrodite at
Od. 8.267-276, are notable exceptions. Some editors believe Apollo
wanted to tie the cattle so he could lead them back to Pieria, but the
parallel they cite for the use of willows to tie animals (*Od.* 9.427) comes
from the description of Odysseus lashing Polyphemos' sheep together
in threes so his men could hide under them.

feet   410
from the very spot, easily twisted together graft-like with each other
and over all the cattle of the fields
by the will of theft-minded Hermes. But Apollo
stood in wonder as he looked on. Then indeed powerful
    Argeiphontes
looked at a spot to the side, darting fire from his eyes,°   415
eager to hide [the deed]. But he easily soothed the farshooting
glorious son of Leto, as he himself wished,
although Apollo was stronger. But taking the lyre in his left hand,
he tried it string by string with the plectrum, and under his hand
it resounded awesomely. And Phoibos Apollo laughed   420
with joy and the lovely sound of the divine music
went through his heart, and a sweet longing took hold of him
in his breast as he listened. But playing sweetly on the lyre
the son of Maia, taking heart, stood to the left
of Phoibos Apollo and soon, as he played clearly on the lyre,   425
he sang in prelude, and lovely was his voice in accompaniment,
as he honored both immortal gods and dark earth, singing
how they first came to be and how each won his portion.°
Mnemosyne° first of the gods he honored with his song,
the mother of the Muses, for she had the son of Maia as her lot.   430

---

415   Again editors suspect a lacuna after this line since there is no
        expressed object for the verb "to hide" in the following line.

428-432 While Hermes' first song was a hymn to himself (57-61), this second
        song is a full theogony, like Hesiod's. Since Hermes sings of the birth
        and acquisition of *timê* for each god in order of age, we can assume
        that the song ends with his own story, and probably a heavy hint to
        Apollo about what domain Hermes wants for himself.

429-430 Mnemosyne, one of the Titans, is the personification of Memory.
        Having slept with Zeus for nine nights in a row, she then bore the nine
        Muses who are the patron goddesses of song and singers (*Th.* 52-63).
        Since early Greek poetry belonged to an oral tradition, this link
        between memory and the Muses who inspired a poet is significant.
        Most poets begin their songs with an invocation to the Muse (e.g. *Il.*
        1.1, *Od.* 1.1, h. *H.* 1.1, *WD* 1, *Th.* 104) but Hermes goes back one
        generation further as if to show that, as a follower of Mnemosyne (and
        part of her domain), he has a greater claim to the realm of music and
        song than Apollo does.

        Why Mnemosyne had Hermes as part of her lot is not explained here,
        nor is it mentioned elsewhere in Greek literature. As a god associated
        with herds and the countryside, Hermes, like Apollo, would have a
        natural connection to the songs and music performed by shepherds
        and inspired by the Muses and their mother. Moreover, as messenger

Then the glorious son of Zeus honored the immortals
according to age and as each had been born,
singing everything in order as he played the lyre upon his arm.

But an irresistible desire took hold of the other's heart in his breast°
and, speaking winged words, Apollo addressed him.   435
"Slayer of cattle, contriver of plots, hard worker, comrade of the feast,
these things you have invented are worth fifty cows.
And so I think we shall settle our differences peacefully hereafter.
But come now, tell me this, resourceful son of Maia,
whether these wonderful deeds have accompanied you
        from birth   440
or some one of the immortals or mortal men
gave them as a glorious gift and taught you this divinely sweet song?
For full of wonder is this newly-revealed sound I am hearing,
a sound which I say no one of men has ever yet learned
nor any of the immortals who have their homes on Olympos   445
far from you, thieving son of Zeus and Maia.
What skill, what music for inescapable cares,
what path? For surely one can take three things together in all:
joy and love and sweet sleep.
For I too am an attendant of the Olympian Muses°   450
who care for dances and the glorious path of song and
rich music and the piercing sound of flutes which stirs longing.
But never have I cared so much in my heart for anything else,
even as clever as the deeds of young men at a feast are.
I marvel, son of Zeus, how beautifully you play these things on the
        lyre.   455
But now since, even though you are little, you know splendid devices,
sit, my friend, and agree in your heart with your elders.

of the gods Hermes would, of course, depend as heavily on the powers
of memory as singers in an oral tradition. So his connection to and
dependence on Mnemosyne is natural. For the apportioning of a god's
domain by lot, see h. *Dem.* 86n.

434   The effect of Hermes' playing and song on Apollo is immediate, calming
his anger and replacing it with desire for the music. Similar powers are
often attributed to music in early Greek literature (e.g. *Th.* 98-103, *Il.*
9.186-191, h. *Ap.* 188-193, *Pindar* P.1.1-12).

450   As the "official" god of music, Apollo is known as a follower of the
Muses (see Fig. 8). That Hermes has invented a kind of music and song
unknown to Apollo is astounding, and the older god immediately°
wants to learn it. Part of the novelty may be that, while the flute player
provides music to accompany others while they dance, the lyre may be
played by the poet himself as he sings.

For there will now be renown among the immortal gods
for you yourself and your mother; and I will say it exactly.
Yes, by this spear of cornel wood° I shall lead the way for you   460
to be famous among the immortals and rich,
and I will give you glorious gifts and I will not deceive you to the
    end."

And Hermes answered him with crafty words.
"You question me very carefully, Far-shooter, but I do not at all
begrudge you entering into my art.   465
You will know this skill today. I want to be conciliatory to you
in thought and words, and you know all this well in your mind.
For you are seated first among the immortals, son of Zeus,
both good and strong. And Zeus the deviser loves you
with all respect, and has given you splendid gifts.   470
And they say, Worker-from-afar, that from the voice of Zeus you
    have learned
both honors and prophecies, all divine pronouncements from Zeus.°
From these things I myself have now learned that I will be a [rich
    boy].°
And it is your own choice to learn whatever skill you want.
But since your heart is so eager to play the lyre,   475
sing and play the lyre and get ready for merriment,
as you receive it from me. But you, friend, grant me glory.°
Holding the clear-voiced companion in your hands, sing well

---

460   As he set out after the cattle thief Apollo apparently took a spear instead
of his customary bow and arrows. Here he swears by this temporary
attribute, as Achilles swore by the sceptre symbolic of a king's power at
Iliad 1.234. There is no obvious significance to the cornel wood itself
which, as a strong and hard kind of wood, may have been commonly
used for spears.

471-472 These lines, which make clear that Apollo has special knowledge of
the *timê* Zeus allots to each god, suggest the reason Hermes chose to
challenge Apollo rather than another god.

473   The Greek text here is unreadable. The translation "rich boy" follows the
nearest guess as to the words in the text, but is not a happy solution. If
correct, though, it may refer to the gains Hermes will receive as a result
of his inventiveness. Apollo has already admitted that the lyre and its
music are worth the fifty cows he stole, and lines 491-494 suggest that
Hermes intends to continue his patronage of herds.

477   Hermes happily gives over the lyre to Apollo since the latter is already
god of music, and Hermes wants his own domain. In exchange for this
gift, Hermes will get the *timê* he has longed for since the opening lines of
the hymn. See lines 491-498.

since you know how to speak beautifully and well in order.
Hereafter, untroubled, take it to the rich feast   480
and the lovely dance and to the glory-loving revel,
a joy both night and day. Whoever inquires into it
knowledgeably, with skill and wisdom,
it will teach, speaking all sorts of things which bring joy to the mind
being played easily with gentle acquaintance   485
as it avoids much-suffering labor. But if someone asks of it
violently at first without knowledge,
then in vain and off key will it sound false notes!
But it is your own choice to learn whatever skill you want.
And I will give you this lyre, glorious son of Zeus,   490
But I in turn will graze the cattle of the fields in pastures
of the mountain and horse-nurturing plain, Worker-from-afar.
Then in great numbers the cows, mating with bulls, will bring forth
both males and females together. And you need not
be violently angry at all, even though you are seeking
        an advantage."   495

So saying he held out the lyre, and Phoibos Apollo received it.
And he put in Hermes' hand the shining whip he held,
and entrusted the tending of cattle to him, and the son of
        Maia took it
laughing. And taking the lyre in his left hand
the glorious son of Leto, Apollo who works from afar,   500
tested it string by string with the plectrum, and under his hand
it resounded awesomely. And the god sang beautifully to it.

Then the two of them turned the cows towards the sacred meadow,
and the splendid children of Zeus themselves
hastened back to snowy Olympos   505
delighting in the lyre, and so Zeus the deviser rejoiced,
and joined them both in friendship. And in this way Hermes
loved the son of Leto continuously as he still does even now,
since he put the longed-for lyre into the Far-shooter's hands
as a token, and the latter played it skillfully on his arm.   510

But Hermes himself in turn sought out the craft of another skill;
he made for himself the sound of shepherd's pipes heard from afar.°

And then the son of Leto spoke to Hermes.

---

512   This instrument was known as "Pan pipes" since Pan, a son of Hermes,
      who spent his time in the woods, became well-known for playing on it.
      In Ovid's account Mercury (Hermes) tells Argus the instrument was
      invented by Pan after the nymph he was chasing (Syrinx) turned into

"I fear, son of Maia, crafty-minded guide,
lest you steal my lyre and my curved bow.°   515
For you have as your domain from Zeus the establishment
of deeds of exchange among men on the nourishing earth.
But if you should venture to swear the great oath of the gods for me,
either nodding with your head or swearing by the rainy water of the
    Styx,°
you would be doing things altogether pleasing
    and dear to my heart."   520
And then the son of Maia nodded, promising
that he would never steal away what the Far-shooter had won,
and that he would never draw near his well-built house. But Apollo,
son of Leto, for the sake of friendship and love nodded
that no one else among the immortals would be more dear,   525
neither god nor mortal born of Zeus. And ... [he said]

. . . .

"I shall make [you?] a token for all the gods and at the same time
trusted and honored in my heart. Then
I shall give you a splendid staff° of wealth and prosperity
made of gold, with three branches, which will guard
    you unharmed,   530
accomplishing all the laws both of words and good deeds,
as many as I claim to know from the voice of Zeus.
But, my friend, cherished by Zeus, it is not ordained by divine will

---

reeds (*Met.* 1.678-712); cf. h. 19.16n., Apollodorus 3.10.2. Hermes'
invention of this new instrument confirms his continued association
with music and with animals of the field. It also shows that he has lost
nothing in giving up the lyre to Apollo

514-515 Since the two gods have already been reconciled, these lines seem
out of place, and have led some editors to suspect that the last seventy
lines or so of the hymn are not original. The tradition that Hermes
stole Apollo's bow is preserved in other versions of the story (e.g.
Horace, *Odes* 1.10.11), and the phrase "my lyre and curved bow"
occurs in almost the same words at h. *Ap.* 131.

519   For the Styx see h. *Ap.* 85n.

529   This is the *kerykeion* (herald's staff) or caduceus which Hermes carries
and uses to put men to sleep or awaken them (*Il.* 24.343-344; *Od.* 24.1-
5). Along with his winged sandals, and traveling cap, this staff is one
of his most common attributes in art. See fig. 6.

535   Although Hermes does not overtly ask for the gift of prophecy, he
does speak of Apollo's art at 471-472 as he prepares to teach his
brother the art of the lyre. His explanations about how to play that
instrument (482-488) are also couched in terms of prophecy, perhaps
containing a hint to which Apollo replies here.

for you or anyone else of the immortals to know the prophetic skill
which you ask about.° For the mind of Zeus knows it. But I,   535
having been trusted, nodded and swore a strong oath
that, apart from me, no one else of the gods who live forever
would know the shrewd will of Zeus.
And you, brother with the golden staff, do not bid me
declare the divine pronouncements which wide-seeing
    Zeus devises.   540
But among men I shall harm one and profit another,
as I perplex the many tribes of wretched men.
And he will enjoy my voice who comes
guided by the cry and flights of birds of sure augury.°
This one will enjoy my voice and I will not deceive him.   545
But whoever, having put his trust in vainly-chattering birds,
comes to seek out my prophecy foolishly,
and to know more than the eternal gods,
I say that he will travel a vain road, but I would take his gifts.

And I will tell you something else, son of glorious Maia   550
and Zeus who bears the aegis, swift spirit° of the gods,
for there are certain holy sisters born,°
maidens delighting in their swift wings,
three of them. And sprinkling themselves on the head with white bar-
    ley meal
they live in homes under the fold of Parnassos,°   555
far-away teachers of a prophetic skill which I practised

---

544   As in Hermes' cautions about using the lyre (482-488), Apollo warns
here (543-549) about the need to use augury (prophecy by the flight of
birds) with care. If a man reads the signs of the birds incorrectly, and
foolishly seeks Apollo's oracle under the wrong auspices or asks an
improper question, he will not get a true answer. This is a good
explanation for so-called "false" prophecies since it places the blame
squarely on man's inability to understand the unerring word of the
gods.

551   The words *daimon* (translated here as "spirit") and *theos* (the usual word
for "god") are used apparently interchangeably for Hermes throughout
the hymn until here. In other early epic *daimon* usually refers to an
unknown god or force influencing the fortune of man, but never to a
specific god. The poet may have used it here to underscore Hermes'
mysterious and crafty power.

552-563 These "bee-maidens" are probably the Thriai, nymphs associated with
a kind of divination through pebbles (*thriai*). How this process worked,
or what these women looked like, remains a mystery. Cf. Apollodorus
3.10.2.

555   Parnassos is the mountain on which Delphi sits. See Map 2.

when I was still a child among the cattle. And my father did
    not bother about this skill.
From there indeed flying one place and another
they feed on honeycombs and accomplish each thing.
But when those eating the yellow honey are inspired,   560
they are willing and eager to speak the truth.
But if they are robbed of the sweet food of the gods,
then indeed do they tell lies, buzzing among one another.
These then I give to you, and as long as you ask them exactly,
delight your heart there. And if you should teach a mortal man, 565
he will listen to your voice often if he is lucky.
Keep these, son of Maia, and the curve-horned cattle of the fields
and take care of horses and mules which endure work ..."°
. . . .
and [he granted] glorious Hermes to be lord over flashing-
    eyed lions
and white-tusked boars and dogs and sheep,   570
as many as the wide earth nourishes, and over all herds,
and to be sole messenger appointed to Hades°
who, although he does not receive gifts, will give by no means the
    least prize of honor.

So lord Apollo loved the son of Maia
with every kind of friendship, and Kronios added grace.   575
And Hermes associates with all mortals and immortals;
sometimes he brings profit, but endlessly he deceives
the tribes of mortal men through the dark night.
    And so farewell, son of Zeus and Maia,
and I will remember you and another song too.   580

---

568   Somewhere in the break after this line Apollo's speech ends and the
        narrative starts up again including a list of the *timai* which Hermes
        will have.
572   Hades is the brother of Zeus to whom the Underworld fell as his lot.
        The name is used both for the god and the place. Hermes' role as
        messenger of Hades means he will lead the souls of dead people down
        to the Underworld, and will carry messages back and forth between
        the living and dead.

5. HYMN TO APHRODITE

Introduction

There is no external evidence with which to fix either the date of the *Hymn to Aphrodite* or its place of origin. The language of the hymn and its relation both to the Hesiodic poems and the *Hymn to Demeter* suggest an origin in the Aeolic tradition and a date around 675 BC, making it the oldest of the surviving long hymns. The love of Aphrodite and Anchises was known both to the Homeric (*Il.* 2.819-821, 5.311-313) and Hesiodic traditions (*Th.* 1008-1010), but no other early versions of this story exist outside of this hymn (cf. Apollodorus 3.12.2; Theocritus 20.34).

Both the humorous tone of the *Hymn to Aphrodite* and its subject matter, which tells of Aphrodite's love affair with the mortal Anchises and foretells the birth of the Trojan hero Aeneas, have made it a favorite among modern audiences. Unlike the other hymns, which show a god or goddess wielding power over others, this one celebrates Aphrodite's power by showing how the goddess of love cannot herself resist love's passion. Zeus, tired of her penchant for making gods fall in love with mortals, "casts sweet longing" in Aphrodite's heart so that she too will make love with a human and bear him a son. It is this union with a mortal, and not her submission to the powers of love *per se*, which causes Aphrodite shame. In the archaic culture of the poem's audience, a person's worth was judged not by internal standards such as honesty, kindness, or wisdom, but by external measures such as how many possessions and thus how much power a person had. In such a hierarchical system (presumably), no immortal would choose *freely* to mate with a mortal. The only way to neutralize Aphrodite's superiority over the other gods, then, is to force her to succumb to her own powers. What keeps the story from being simply a mean-spirited tale of revenge is that, while being a victim of Zeus' trick, Aphrodite is at the same time portrayed as the seducer in her affair with Anchises. The power of desire may lead her to an unworthy lover but, even so, love is sweet.

Like the Homeric *Hymn to Demeter*, this hymn also involves a tension between mortality and immortality, as well as a battle of wills between Zeus and a goddess. Zeus puts an end to Aphrodite's mating of gods with mortals by turning the goddess' power on herself. Anchises fears retribution when he realizes he has slept with a goddess but, with the examples of Ganymede and Tithonos, Aphrodite reassures him of the gods' goodwill toward his whole family. These examples at the same time illustrate and confirm the gulf that exists between mortals and the gods. Zeus granted Ganymede eternal youth and immortality. However Eos, the goddess of dawn, could not do the same for her mortal lover, who received eternal life but continued to grow older and more infirm each day. Aphrodite's pledge to Anchises shows she will not put him in that grey area between mortal and god, but she also makes clear, though implicitly, that she will not seek for him a grant of eternal youth and immortality from Zeus. This done, Aphrodite bows tacitly to the power of Zeus, with the concession that she will no longer force immortals to mate with mortals. The poem ends with the goddess' warning that Anchises not reveal her identity as the mother of his son, and with her return to the heavens. The hymn celebrates the power of Aphrodite, while at the same time reinforcing her subordinate place to Zeus in the divine sphere and confirming the natural distinction between mortals and immortals.

Although the hymn does not tell the story of Aphrodite's birth and acquisition of power over sexual love, in many places it assumes the listener's (or reader's) familiarity with this background. Many of the goddess' epithets are derived from the story of her birth, and her erotic power itself is linked closely to her origins. In the *Theogony* of Hesiod, one of the first elements of the cosmos is an abstract figure called Eros, the embodiment of desire, who has no distinct mythology. This figure is replaced in the generation of the Olympian gods by the the female figure of Aphrodite, who plays an active role in many myths. The story of Aphrodite's birth in Hesiod (*Th.* 188-200) and its allusions in the Aphrodite hymn provide a good example of the aetiological connection between myth and cult. The first part of the Hesiodic story (*Th.* 154-187) explains an observable phenomenon of nature, the placement of the sky high above the earth, by personifying those elements of nature as male and female deities. The sky god, Ouranos, used to lie directly on top of the earth, a goddess named Gaia. As a result, children were created but also prevented from being born, since their father constantly pushed them back into their mother's womb. Gaia, understandably unhappy with this situation, plotted to overthrow her husband. She concealed from him the birth of a son, Kronos, who grew up and, with her help, castrated his father, Ouranos, thus ending the constant intercourse between Ouranos and Gaia. This violent deed caused the eternal separation of earth and sky.

The next part of the same story provides an explanation for the origins and nature of Aphrodite as the Greek goddess of desire and sexual love, who was also known in cult by the names "Ourania," "Kytherea " and "Cypris": the title "Ourania" implies that she was the daughter of Ouranos, while the name Aphrodite, which contains the Greek word for sea-foam (*aphros*), implies an origin in the sea. The myth easily reconciles these conflicting titles by telling how, after Kronos' attack, the male sex organs of Ouranos fell into the ocean where they were surrounded by the foam out of which Aphrodite eventually emerged. The last two titles imply connections with the islands of Kythera and Cyprus (where important shrines to the goddess existed in antiquity), so in the myth the foam floats first past Kythera and finally to Cyprus before the goddess is born.

HYMN TO APHRODITE

Muse, sing to me the deeds of golden Aphrodite
of Cyprus,° who roused sweet longing in the gods
and overwhelmed the tribes of mortal men
and the birds of the air and all the beasts,
as many as the land nourishes and the sea;   5
for the deeds of fair-wreathed Kytherea° are a care to all.

But three minds she cannot persuade or deceive:°

1	The "deeds of Aphrodite" refer not just to her actions, but also to the goddess' sphere of influence: sexual love. The same Greek word (*ergon*) is used often of a god's domain, e.g. in line 10 where it describes war as the "work of Ares " and again in lines 11 and 15 of Athena's patronage of handicraft.
	Unlike the other hymns which open with a focus on the deity, this hymn announces that its subject will be the goddess' domain: sex. Because we know that a hymn celebrates the power of the god or goddess it praises, we expect an account of how Aphrodite influences others to fall in love. What we get, however, is the story of her own helpless submission to the powers of love and passion. See also 7-33n. below.
2	Aphrodite's connection with Cyprus in myth stems from the story of her birth in the sea-foam which carried her to shore on that island; see h. 6.5n. For this reason her most common epithet in early poetry is *Cypris*. Her cult associations with the island are equally strong: a temple to her was built at Paphos, on the western end of Cyprus in the 12th c. BC, and another was added in the archaic period. The origin of the goddess and her cult is not known, although she seems to be associated with the Phoenician goddess, Ishtar-Astarte, whose worship on the island of Cyprus was established at least by the end of the 9th century.
6	*Kytherea* is another common name for Aphrodite. According to Hesiod's account of her birth (*Th*.188-200), she floated by the island of Kythera (just off the southern coast of the Peloponnese, see Maps 1, 2) before coming ashore on Cyprus. Kythera was also the site of one of her oldest shrines, perhaps founded by Phoenicians.
7-33	In a nice ring composition, the poet singles out the only three deities who are immune to Aphrodite's power: Athena (8-15), Artemis (16-20), and Hestia (21-32). Just as line 7 introduces this section, line 33 will repeat "she cannot persuade the minds of these [three goddesses]." This section on the three virgin goddesses helps to define Aphrodite through her contrast

the daughter of aegis-bearing Zeus, grey-eyed Athena;
for the deeds of golden Aphrodite do not bring her joy,
but wars are pleasing to her, and the work of Ares,   10
and battle songs and preparing glorious deeds.
She first taught earth-dwelling craftsmen
to make carriages and chariots intricately worked with bronze;
and the soft-skinned maidens in the halls
she taught glorious deeds, by placing skill in the minds of each.   15

Nor does laughter-loving° Aphrodite ever tame in love
loud-crying Artemis of the golden bow.
For bow and arrows are her joy and slaying wild beasts in the mountains,
and lyres and choruses and piercing cries
and shady groves and the city of righteous men.   20

Nor do the deeds of Aphrodite bring joy to the reverent maiden,
Hestia,° whom crafty-minded Kronos° begot first,
and also the last born, by the plan of Zeus who bears the aegis,

---

with them. At the same time it refines a theme introduced in lines 2-3, which stress her power over all creatures, both mortal and immortal. There the poet tells us she "overwhelms" her subjects by "rousing sweet desire" in them. In line 7 we learn that the fulfillment of love's passion comes not through force, but by the gentler arts of persuasion and even deception. Throughout the hymn and elsewhere in Greek poetry, Aphrodite and the love she inspires are consistently described in terms of seduction, sweetness, and joy. Thus when these very charms are turned against the goddess by Zeus in the story of this hymn, there is no sense of outrage at an unwanted conquest. The delights of love are simply so great that not even the goddess who is said to control them can resist their persuasion. And so, after all, it is fitting that the hymnist has chosen the more powerful of the two as his subject.

16   "Laughter-loving" is one of Aphrodite's most common epithets in early epic (*Il.* 3.424, *Od.* 6.362). Hesiod plays with the similar sound of the roots for "laughter" *meid* and "genitals" *medea* to link this epithet with the story of Aphrodite's birth (*Th.* 200); see introductory note.

22-23 In Hesiod's account (*Th.* 454) Hestia is the eldest daughter of Kronos and Rhea and is immediately swallowed by Kronos, who subjects each of his newborn children to this fate in an effort to avoid being deposed by one of them, as a prophecy has foretold. However, Rhea deceives him at Zeus' birth by substituting for the infant a stone which Kronos swallows in ignorance. Zeus then grows up to overthrow Kronos and force him to disgorge the rest of his offspring in reverse order of their birth, beginning with the stone he had swallowed last (*Th.* 493-497) and ending with his first-born, Hestia. She thus becomes his last-born and youngest child, although begotten first. See genealogical chart.

22   It is likely that Kronos' epithet *ankulometes*, "crafty-minded," originally meant Kronos "of the curved sickle," in reference to his castration of

an august goddess, whom Poseidon and Apollo courted,
but she was altogether unwilling and steadfastly refused.   25
She touched the head of father Zeus,° the aegis-bearer,
and swore a great oath which was fulfilled
that she would be a virgin all her days, shining among goddesses.
And father Zeus granted her a noble prize of honor in place of
    marriage
and so she sat in the middle of the house,° having chosen the richest
    prize.   30
In all the temples of the gods she is the holder of honor°
and among all mortals she is honored as the eldest of the gods.

Of these [three goddesses] she cannot persuade their minds nor
deceive them.
But for the rest there is no escaping Aphrodite,
neither for blessed gods nor mortal men.   35
She even led astray the mind of Zeus who delights in the
    thunderbolt,°
he who is the greatest and has the greatest share of honor.

Ouranos. Hesiod's application of the epithet to Prometheus, however, shows that the sense "of the bent mind" (*mêtis*) was already understood by his time.

26   One of Zeus' common epithets as the supreme ruler is "father of gods and men," but the abbreviated version which appears here, "father Zeus," is also common (e.g. h. *Dem.* 321, h. *Ap.* 307, h. *H.* 368). On the aegis see h. *H.* 183n.

30   Hestia was the goddess of the hearth, which was placed in the center of each house and was the focal point of daily worship in the home. As the next line implies, each temple also had a hearth on which sacrifices could be made, so Hestia held a share of honor in the sanctuaries of all the gods as well. For the Romans, Hestia became the goddess Vesta, whose temple was cared for by the Vestal Virgins. See h. 29.

31   The Greek adjective (*timaochos*) appears only here and at h. *Dem.* 268. Other similar correspondences between the poems suggest the Aphrodite hymn influenced that to Demeter.

36   Anyone familiar with Greek mythology and Zeus' long list of extramarital affairs will not think this a great feat but, at least theoretically, the praise of Aphrodite's power is enhanced by her control over the king of all gods and men. A partial catalogue of his affairs is given to Hera by Zeus himself at *Il.* 14.315-328.
Lines 40-45 here are given over to praise of Hera, as if to forestall any jealousy on her part. Hera is described as the most beautiful of the goddesses in a physical sense (41), but in spite of her beauty it is Aphrodite who has the more powerful seductive charm. In Homer these attributes are symbolized by an embroidered band of Aphrodite's clothing which Hera borrows at *Il.* 14.214-223 when she wishes to seduce Zeus herself.

And, whenever she wished, deceiving his wise mind,
she easily mated him with mortal women,
making him completely forget Hera, his sister and wife,   40
who is by far the best in form among the immortal goddesses,
and the most glorious child born to crafty-minded Kronos
and mother Rhea. And Zeus, who knows imperishable plans,
made her his revered, devoted wife.

But even in the heart of Aphrodite herself Zeus cast sweet longing 45
to make love with a mortal man, so that soon
not even she would be kept from the bed of a mortal
and so that one day, boasting among all the gods, laughing sweetly,
she would not tell how laughter-loving Aphrodite
had mated gods to mortal women,   50
and they had borne mortal sons to the immortals,
and how she had mated goddesses to mortal men.

So he cast in her heart sweet longing for Anchises,°
who, at that time, like the immortals in build, was tending cattle
on the lofty peaks of Mt. Ida rich in springs.°   55
Then indeed, seeing him, laughter-loving Aphrodite
was struck with love, and astounding desire seized her heart.

To Cyprus she went and entered her fragrant temple
at Paphos where her sacred precinct was and her fragrant altar.
There she went inside and shut the gleaming doors.°   60

---

53   Anchises was a Trojan prince descended from king Tros (cf. line 208), who
      gave his name to the city of Troy and its people. Anchises, a cousin of the
      Trojan king Priam, is important in mythology chiefly as the father of
      Aeneas, and is best known from this myth and Vergil's *Aeneid*.

55   Mt. Ida is located southeast of the city of Troy in Asia Minor (see Map 1).
      It is also the site of another famous seduction scene, in which Hera
      deceives and seduces Zeus in order to distract him from the gods'
      meddling on the battlefield at Troy. That story, told at *Il*. 14.153-360, is
      similar to this hymn in many respects, and worth reading in its own right.

60-63 In early epic a typical prelude to battle is the scene of a warrior arming
      himself. This scene is of exactly the same type, as Aphrodite literally arms
      herself for love. Cf. *Il*. 14.169-186, and h. 6.5-13. In this case the remaining
      description of Aphrodite's appearance is delayed until lines 86-90 when
      we see her through the eyes of Anchises. See also h. *Aph*. 89n.

And the Graces° bathed her and anointed her
with ambrosial olive oil, such as is poured over the gods who are for-
     ever,
divinely sweet, which was made fragrant for her.°
Having clothed herself well in all her beautiful robes
adorned with gold, laughter-loving Aphrodite   65
hastened to Troy, leaving behind sweet-smelling Cyprus,
swiftly making her way high up among the clouds.

She came to Ida rich in springs, mother of beasts,
and went straight to the shepherd's hut across the mountain.
And fawning after her leapt grey wolves and flashing-eyed lions,   70
bears and swift leopards hungry for deer.
Seeing them she rejoiced in her heart
and cast longing in their breasts, and together they all
lay down in pairs in their shadowy lairs.°

But she herself came to the well-built shelters   75
and found him left alone at the huts by the others,
Anchises, the hero, who had beauty from the gods.
All the others followed their cattle along the grassy pastures,
but he, left alone at the huts by the others,
was walking here and there playing clearly on the lyre.   80
Aphrodite, the daughter of Zeus, stood in front of him
like an unmarried maiden in form and stature,
so that he would not be afraid when he saw her with his eyes.
And Anchises looking, saw her and marveled
at her form and stature and shining clothes.°   85

---

61   The Graces (*Charites*) were the three daughters of Zeus and Eurynome (a
      daughter of Okeanos): *Aglaia* ("Splendor"), *Euphrosyne* ("Happiness"),
      and *Thalia* ("Good Cheer"). They, along with the *Horai* ("Seasons"),
      were frequent attendants of Aphrodite. Cf. h. 6.5.

63   The olive oil mentioned here was made fragrant with aromatics such
      as rose and sage so that it acted as a perfume. Hera too uses perfumed
      oil as she prepares to meet Zeus (*Il.* 14.171-174). Oil was not only
      rubbed on the skin and hair (cf. h. 24.3n), but seems to have been used
      on clothing as well (cf. 85n. below).

70-74 Aphrodite's power over animals, mentioned in lines 4-5, is illustrated
      here where the presence of the goddess causes them to mate.
      Lucretius, in *De Rerum Natura* 1.10-20, describes a similar scene to
      illustrate the spell cast by the goddess Venus over all creatures and the
      fertility she brings to the earth. Cf. also Kirke in *Odyssey* 10.

85   The adjective translated here as "shining" is a standard epithet for
      clothes (also at 164; cf. *Il.* 3.419 for a similar phrase), and has puzzled

For she wore a robe more brilliant than the bright light of fire,
and she had on spiral bracelets and bright earrings
and around her soft neck were beautiful necklaces,
lovely, golden, intricately worked. Like the moon°
a radiance shone around her soft breasts, a wonder to see.   90

Desire seized Anchises and he spoke to her,
"Hail lady,° whoever of the blessed gods you are, who has come to
    this house,
Artemis or Leto or golden Aphrodite
or well-born Themis or grey-eyed Athena
or perhaps one of the Graces come here, who are companions   95
to all the gods and are called immortal,
or one of the nymphs who live in the beautiful woods
or the nymphs who inhabit this beautiful mountain
and the springs of its rivers and the grassy meadows.
For you on a mountain peak, in a place visible from all around,   100
I will make an altar, and I will offer fair sacrifices
in all seasons. And you, keeping a kindly spirit,
grant that among the Trojans I may be a distinguished man

---

many readers of the Homeric poems. The best explanation is that the
olive oil used in the manufacture of wool and linen (to soften and
perfume the cloth) caused a glossy appearance. Evidence for this idea is
contained in several different sources, including Linear B tablets which
list allotments of oil to weavers and finishers, (one even designates "oil
to Potnia [a goddess] as unguent for cloth"), Homer (*Il.* 18.596-597, of
chitons "dripping with oil," *Od.* 7. 105-107, of oil dripping from cloth as
it is woven), and even a Middle Bronze Age tablet from Mari (Syria)
which talks explicitly of "[sesame] oil to make cloth shine." See further
in C. W. Shelmerdine, "Shining and Fragrant Cloth in Homer," in J.
Carter and S. Morris eds., *The Ages of Homer* (Austin 1995).

89   A Sumerian hymn describes the goddess Inanna also appearing to her
     lover "like the light of the moon." The same hymn, which includes an
     account of Inanna's preparations (bathing, anointing, dressing, putting
     on jewelry) provides an ancient parallel for the ornaments worn by
     Aphrodite in her seduction scenes.

92-106 When Odysseus first sees Nausikaä in the *Odyssey* (6.149-154), he too
     begins his speech by comparing her to a goddess. But the bulk of the
     address makes clear that he wishes to flatter her and knows full well
     that she is a mortal. Anchises, on the other hand, seems genuinely awe-
     struck by the beauty of the young woman before him, and addresses her
     as a goddess throughout his speech. Not knowing exactly which
     goddess she is and not wishing to offend, he carefully lists all the likely
     candidates, then offers to build her an altar, and closes with a prayer
     that he live to a ripe old age, blessed with successful offspring and

and make my offspring flourish in the future. But for myself let me
live well for a long time and see the light of the sun   105
blessed among my people and reach the threshold of old age."

Then Aphrodite, the daughter of Zeus, answered him,°
"Anchises, most glorious of men born on the earth,
I am not a god. Why do you compare me to the immortals?
I am mortal, and the mother who bore me was a woman.   110
Otreus is my father, a glorious name, if you have perhaps heard it,
who is lord of all well-fortified Phrygia.°
Your language and my own I know well,
for a Trojan nurse reared me in my house. She took me
from my dear mother as a small child and raised me.   115
So indeed I know your language well too.
But now Argeiphontes of the golden staff snatched me up
from the dance of loud-crying Artemis of the golden bow.°
There were many of us nymphs and much-courted° maidens
dancing, and a boundless company circled around us.   120

honored among his people. This offer and his final prayer betray
Anchises' fear that, having seen her, he may have offended the deity and
put his life at risk.

Aphrodite's divine beauty and sexual appeal shine through her disguise
here, just as at *Iliad* 3.396-399 where Helen recognizes the goddess despite
her appearance as an old woman. Cf. h. *Dem.* 188-189 where the disguised
Demeter nonetheless shows flashes of her divinity.

107-142 Although Anchises has already been captivated by her beauty,
Aphrodite uses both persuasion and deception (cf. line 7) in this speech to
seduce him. According to her story, not only is she a virgin born to noble
parents who will pay a fine dowry, but even the gods have decreed that
Anchises take her as his wife. Her lying tale contains just enough detail
(e.g. her father's name, the reason she can speak Anchises' language —
see below) to be convincing, and is typical of other such tales in early epic.
Cf. the lying tales of Odysseus in the *Odyssey*. For lies by other deities, see
the hymns to Demeter and to Hermes

112-116 Phrygia was an area of Asia Minor to the west and north of Troy (see
Map 1), and their king Otreus fought with Priam, king of Troy, against the
Amazons (*Il.* 3.184-189). We know from *Iliad* 4. 437-438 that those fighting
at Troy did not share a common language, and Aphrodite embellishes her
outright lie here with the believable detail that she learned the Trojan
tongue from her nurse.

117-118 On Argeiphontes (= Hermes see h. *H.* 73n. For the theme of girls
abducted while dancing see h. *Dem.* 5n.

119   The epithet's literal meaning, "earning oxen," refers to the bride price a
suitor would pay to the parents of his chosen wife. This phrase establishes
her as a maiden ready for marriage (like Nausikaä in the *Odyssey*) and
looks ahead to her (supposed) concern for the proper performance of the
marriage rites (131-141).

Then Argeiphontes of the golden staff snatched me,
and led me over many fields of mortal men,
many poor and untilled, through which wild beasts,
eaters of raw flesh, roam along their shadowy haunts,
and I did not think I would touch the life-giving earth
    with my feet.   125
He kept saying that in the bed of Anchises I would be called
your wedded wife, and that I would bear you glorious children.
But when indeed he had explained and told me this, again
the strong Argeiphontes went away among the tribes of
    the immortals.
So I have come to you, and a strong compulsion is upon me.   130
I beg you, by Zeus and by your parents,
noble people, (for base ones would not have borne such a son),
take me untouched and inexperienced in love
and show me to your father and devoted mother
and to your brothers who were born from the same womb.   135
I will not be an unfitting daughter- or sister-in-law for them, but a
    seemly one.
Send a messenger quickly to the Phrygians with their swift horses
to tell my father and my worried mother.
And if you do, they will send abundant gold and woven clothing,
and you accept their many splendid dowry gifts!   140
And after you have done these things, arrange a lovely wedding feast
held in honor by men and immortal gods."

Speaking thus the goddess cast sweet longing in his heart.
And desire took hold of Anchises and he said,
"If you are mortal and a mortal woman was your mother,°   145
and Otreus is your father, a glorious name, as you say,
and if you have come here by the grace of the immortal guide,
Hermes, and you are to be called my wife forever after,
then no one of the gods or of mortal men
will restrain me until I have made love with you here   150
now at once; not even if the far-shooter himself, Apollo,

145-154 Like Hermes who insists (*Od.* 8.339-342) he would gladly endure the
    public ridicule of all the gods watching if only he could share
    Aphrodite's bed, Anchises too is willing to pay any price for a moment
    of love with the woman before him. Not realizing that it is he who is
    being seduced, an eager Anchises now seeks to persuade the
    "innocent" Aphrodite to sleep with him right away, since they are to
    be married anyhow! And Aphrodite continues her deception by
    "allowing" him to lead her to his bed and disrobe her.

should shoot his painful arrows from his silver bow.
Then I would be willing, lady like the gods,
after I have entered your bed, to go into the house of Hades."

So speaking he took her hand, and laughter-loving Aphrodite   155
turned, her beautiful eyes cast down, and went
to the well-covered bed, which was already spread
with soft coverings for its lord. And upon it
lay the hides of bears and loud-roaring lions
which he himself had killed on the high mountains.   160
Then when they had climbed onto the well-made bed,
Anchises first took from her skin the gleaming jewelry,
the pins and spiral bracelets and earrings and necklaces.
And he loosened her belt and took off her shining robes
and placed them on a silver-studded chair.   165
Then by the will of the gods and by destiny,
he lay beside the immortal goddess, a mortal, not knowing clearly
    what he did.

But at the time when shepherds turn their cattle and well-grown
    sheep
back to the fold from the flowering pastures,
then she poured on Anchises sweet, refreshing   170
sleep, but she herself put on her beautiful clothes.
And when she was fully clothed the shining goddess
stood in the hut and her head touched
the well-made roof-beam,° and from her cheeks shone
an immortal beauty, the sort which belongs to fair-wreathed
    Kytherea   175
And she woke him from his sleep and said,

"Up, son of Dardanos.° Why do you sleep so soundly?
And consider if I seem to be the same
as when you first saw me with your eyes."

So she spoke and he, from his sleep, reacted quickly.   180
But when he saw the neck and beautiful eyes of Aphrodite
he was afraid and turned his eyes aside in another direction.
Then he covered his noble face with his cloak

173-174 For this characteristic description of the goddess' epiphany cf. h.
       Dem. 189n.
177   The phrase "son of" here is used loosely to mean "descendant of,"
       since Anchises was actually the great-great-grandson of Dardanos.
       Dardanos, a son of Zeus by a mortal woman, was the founder of the
       Trojan line which tooks its name from Dardanos' son, Tros (cf. 53n.).

and spoke winged words° begging her,

"The first minute I saw you with my eyes, goddess,   185
I knew you were a god. But you did not tell the truth.
By Zeus who bears the aegis I beg you,
do not let me live without strength among men
but have pity, since the man is not strong
who sleeps with immortal goddesses."°   190

Then Aphrodite, daughter of Zeus, answered him,
"Anchises, most noble of mortal men,
have courage and do not fear too much in your heart.
For you should have no fear that you will suffer harm from me
or from the other blessed ones, since you are dear to the gods.   195
You will have a dear son who will be a lord among the Trojans
and children will continue to be born to children.
And his name will be Aeneas, since dreadful
grief held me because I fell into the bed of a mortal man.°
But among mortal men those of your race   200
have always been especially close to the gods in form and stature.

Indeed Zeus the deviser snatched up golden-haired Ganymede

---

184   The meaning of this common Homeric formula, "s/he spoke winged/
      feathered words" (appearing 55 times in the *Iliad* and 60 times in the
      Odyssey), has been the subject of much debate. The image probably
      comes from that of an arrow which flies straight because of its
      feathers. Thus, words once spoken move through the air from speaker
      to hearer like an arrow. Some scholars see instead the metaphor of a
      bird flying rapidly through the air.
187-190 Anchises has (at least) two reasons to fear the consequences of his
      passion. The language here suggests that he fears Aphrodite will make
      him impotent. In addition, recalling his challenge to fight any god who
      stood in his way (149-154), Anchises may also fear retribution for
      hubris (cf. h. *Ap.* 67n, 541n). Greek mythology is full of examples of
      mortal lovers of an immortal who are punished, either for their *hubris*
      (e.g. Tityos, Ixion), or through the jealousy of another god (e.g.
      Semele). Since Aphrodite was, in fact, the seducer in this case,
      Anchises has no need to fear. Cf. also Odysseus' caution when Kirke
      invites him into her bed (*Od.* 10.333-344).
198-199 The poet puns on the name "Aeneas" here by connecting it to the
      Greek word meaning "dread" (*ainos*). In a conventional ring-
      composition, the hymnist returns to the theme of Aphrodite's grief
      (247) after giving the examples of Ganymede and Tithonos which
      follow. On Aphrodite's grief over this affair, see the introduction to this
      hymn.
202-217 According to the *Iliad* (5.265-66; 20.230-235) Ganymede, the son of

because of his beauty to live among the immortals
and pour wine for the gods in the house of Zeus,
a wonder to see, honored by all the immortals   205
as he draws the red nectar from a golden bowl.
But unending grief held the heart of Tros, and he had no idea
where the divine whirlwind had taken his dear son.
So he kept mourning for him continually all his days.
And Zeus pitied him and gave him as ransom for his son   210
high-stepping horses such as carry the immortals.
These he gave to him to have as a gift. And the guide, Argeiphontes,
told him everything at the command of Zeus,
how Ganymede would be immortal and ageless like the gods.
When indeed he had heard the message of Zeus   215
no longer then did he keep mourning, but he rejoiced in his heart
and rejoicing was carried by the storm-footed° horses.

So too did golden-throned Eos snatch up Tithonos,°
one of your race, a man like the immortals.

---

the Trojan king Tros, was taken up into the heavens by the rest of the gods to be Zeus' cup-bearer. The more common version of the myth (and the one preserved here) has Zeus himself, captivated by the boy's beauty, abduct Ganymede. Although the context of this parallel in the hymn clearly involves erotic love, the hymnist does not speak directly of an erotic relationship between Zeus and Ganymede. The first clear reference to the two as lovers is in Ibykos fr. 289 (6th c. BC).

Like Demeter when her daughter is taken by Hades (cf. h. *Dem.*), Tros grieves until a reconciliation is effected. In this case, Zeus' gift of the divine horses takes the place of the dowry gift ordinarily given to the father of a bride. On other abduction stories of this sort see the introduction to the *Demeter Hymn*.

Ganymede is the first of two examples Aphrodite will give to illustrate cases of a god loving a mortal member of Anchises' race. At line 214 she gives an important detail of the story: although born a mortal, Ganymede receives the gift of immortality and eternal youth from Zeus. See below on 218-238.

217 I.e. swift as the wind.

218 Eos, a daughter of Hyperion and Theia (see genealogical chart), is the goddess of dawn. Her epithets "gold-throned" and "early-born" reflect her role as a deity connected with the first light of the day.

218-238 Tithonos, the second of Aphrodite's examples, was son of Laomedon and brother of Priam. He comes to be identified as the father of Eos' son, Memnon, in some sources (e.g. *Th.* 984) although there is no mention here or in Homer of his fathering any children. Unlike Ganymede who was destined to be eternally young, Tithonos receives immortality without the gift of agelessness and, in the end, lives a life

She went to ask the dark-clouded son of Kronos   220
that he be immortal and live forever.
And Zeus nodded to her and fulfilled her wish.
Foolish mistress Eos did not think in her mind
to ask for youth and to scrape painful old age from him.
And indeed as long as much-desired youth held him,   225
delighting in early-born Eos of the golden throne,
he lived by the flow of Okeanos at the ends of the earth.
But when the first grey hairs flowed down
from his beautiful head and noble chin,
then indeed did queenly Eos keep away from his bed,   230
though she nourished him with food and ambrosia,°
keeping him in her great halls and giving him beautiful clothing.
But when indeed hateful old age bore down upon him altogether
and he couldn't move any of his limbs not even to raise one,
this plan seemed best to her in her heart: 235
she put him away in a chamber and shut the gleaming doors.
There his voice flows on unceasingly and there is no strength at all
as there once was in his flexible limbs.

But I would not choose such a fate for you among the immortals,
to be immortal and to live forever.   240
But if, remaining as you are now in form and figure,
you could live on and be called my husband,
then grief would not enfold my wise heart.
But soon now pitiless old age will enfold you,°
the leveller which, in the end, stands beside men,   245
deadly, wearying, hated even by the gods.

But for me there will be great shame among the immortal gods
forever without end because of you.
Before they used to fear my talk and my schemes, by which at one
      time
I mated all the immortals to mortal women.   250

---

of eternal old age. Later tradition reports the metamorphoses of Tithonos into a cicada, but that version of the myth is not alluded to in the hymn. For Eos with the young Tithonos, see fig. 9.

231 The combination of mortal nourishment (food, "grain") with divine (ambrosia) highlights Tithonos' uncertain status between the gods and men, unable to die but still subject to the mortal aging process.

244 Aphrodite could presumably have asked Zeus to allow Anchises an immortal and ageless existence (like Ganymede), but she does not, and instead stresses the inevitability of the aging process for her mortal lover. For an exploration of the reasons for this, see Smith (1981).

For my will overpowered them all.
But now indeed no longer will my mouth be able to mention
this among the immortals, since I was struck by a great blindness,
wretched and unspeakable, and was driven out of my mind,
and conceived a child in my womb by mating with a mortal.   255

When indeed he first sees the light of the sun,
the deep-bosomed mountain nymphs who dwell
on this great and sacred mountain will raise him.°
They belong neither among mortals nor immortals;
they live for a long time and eat ambrosial food,   260
and they tread the lovely dance among the immortals.
But with them both the Silenoi and sharp-eyed Argeiphontes°
mingle in love in the recesses of lovely caves.
And together with the nymphs, at their birth, firs
or towering oaks grow upon the fruitful earth   265
beautiful, flourishing on the lofty mountains.
They stand high, and people call them sacred groves
of the immortals, and mortals do not cut them at all with an axe.
But whenever the fate of death stands near,
first these beautiful trees wither on the earth,   270
and their bark decays, and their branches fall off,
and at the same time the soul [of nymph and tree] leaves the light of
     the sun.
These nymphs will keep my son with them and raise him.

When he first reaches sweet youth
the goddesses will bring him here and show you your child.°   275
But, so that I may tell you everything in my mind,
I will come again in the fifth year bringing your son.

257-273 These lines describe in some detail the nymphs who will serve as
     Aeneas' nurses. That the hymnist places them explicitly between the
     realms of mortal and immortal is important, for they mediate the
     opposition between mortality and immortality that is at the core of
     Anchises' encounter with Aphrodite (as it is between Ganymede and
     Zeus and Tithonos and Eos). They illustrate as well the continuity of
     life that characterizes both the renewal of the forest and the
     preservation, through the birth of children, of mortal life.

262   The Silenoi seem to have been older satyrs, spirits of nature, who were
     part human, part animal, often shown in vase painting with the legs
     and tail of a goat, and always in a state of sexual arousal. See fig. 10.
     On Argeiphontes (= Hermes) see h. *H* 73n.

274-275 These lines provide a transition between the description of the
     nymphs and the prophecy of Aphrodite, but they seem unnecessarily

Indeed when you first see this young shoot with your eyes,
you will rejoice at the sight, for he will be so much like a god;
and you will take him at once to windy Ilion°   280
And if anyone of mortal men should ask you
what mother conceived your dear son in her womb,
remember to speak to him as I bid you:
"They say he is the offspring of a blushing nymph
one of those who inhabit this tree-covered mountain."   285

But if you should speak out and boast with a foolish mind
that you mingled in love with fair-wreathed Kytherea,
Zeus in his anger will strike you with his smoking thunderbolt.°
Everything has been explained to you. And you, knowing it in your
      mind,
hold back and do not name me, but respect the anger
      of the gods."   290
Having said this she darted up to the windy sky.

Hail goddess who rules well-built Cyprus.
Having begun with you I will move on to another song.

redundant given 277-279. The term "goddesses" in 275 is also
problematic and has led some critics to believe 274-275 are an
interpolation added to the manuscripts by a later scribe.
280 Ilion = Troy
288 According to Hyginus (*Fab.* 94), Anchises did boast and was struck
blind by lightning.

6. HYMN TO APHRODITE

I will sing of beautiful golden-wreathed Aphrodite
the reverent goddess who received as her lot the towers of all
Cyprus on the sea where the moist force of the West wind as it blew
carried her over the waves of the loud-roaring sea
on the soft foam.° And the Horai° with their golden diadems   5
received her happily and wrapped divine clothing around her,
and on her immortal head they placed a well-wrought crown,
beautiful, made of gold, and in her pierced ears
they put flowers of copper and precious gold.
Around her delicate neck and white breasts   10
they adorned her with golden necklaces like those the golden-
      crowned
Horai themselves wear whenever they go
to the lovely dance of the gods and to the house of their father.
But when indeed they had put all the jewelry on her body,
they led her to the immortals, who welcomed her when
      they saw her   15

HYMN TO APHRODITE   We know nothing about the date or place of
      composition of this hymn except that, according to lines 19-20, it was
      composed for performance at a competition.
5a   This account of Aphrodite's birth in the sea and her subsequent trip
      over the waves to Cyprus accords with that told in Hesiod's *Theogony*
      188-200. There, after Kronos castrates his father Ouranos, the latter's
      genitals fall into the sea where they are surrounded by the sea-foam.
      From this union is born Aphrodite, whose name is thus connected by
      popular etymology to the Greek word for the foam (*aphros*) in which she
      was formed and carried to shore at Cyprus; see introductory note to
      Hymn to Aphrodite. In Homer, Aphrodite is the product of a more natural
      union between Zeus and the goddess Dione (*Il.* 5.312). In art, however,
      the image of the new goddess rising from the sea has been a popular
      subject from the Archaic period to Botticelli's *Birth of Venus* and beyond.
5b   The Horai are personifications of the Seasons worshipped in Attic cult
      under the names *Thallo* ("Growth"), *Karpo* ("Flowering"), and, perhaps,
      Auxo ("Ripeness"), but treated as daughters of Zeus and Themis in
      Hesiod's *Theogony* (901-902), where they are called *Eunomia* ("Good

---

and offered their hands in greeting. And each one prayed
that she would be his lawful wife and that he would take her to his
    home,
as they marveled at the beauty of violet-crowned Kytherea.°

Hail, quick-glancing, honey-sweet goddess; grant that I
may carry off the victory in the contest, and inspire my song.   20
And I will remember you and another song.°

7. HYMN TO DIONYSOS

Of Dionysos, son of glorious Semele,°
I shall remember how he appeared along the shore of the barren sea
on a jutting headland, looking like a young man
in the first bloom of youth. And his beautiful dark hair
waved about him, and he wore on his strong shoulders   5
a purple cloak.° Soon men on a well-constructed ship

Government"), *Dikê* ("Justice"), and *Eirene* ("Peace"); see genealogical
chart. In the *Works and Days* (73-75) the *Horai* and the *Charites*
("Graces") both help to clothe and adorn Pandora. Cf. h. *Aph.* 61ff.,
86ff. where it is the Graces who dress Aphrodite and *Cypria* fr. 4 where
Aphrodite dresses herself in garments made by the Horai and Graces.
In Greek art the Horai appear first on the François vase (ca. 560 BC).

18   On Kytherea see h. *Aph.* 6n.

21   This line is a regular formula for the end of a hymn. Cf. h. *Dem* 495,
with note.

HYMN TO DIONYSOS   We have no evidence for the geographical origin
of this hymn and very little on which to base the date of its
composition. Attempts to prove a 5th-century or later date for the
hymn have rested largely on "stylistic" grounds and on the
identification of the Tyrsenians (line 8), but a date in the seventh or
sixth century BC seems more likely on grounds of diction. The story of
Dionysos' attempted abduction by pirates appears in many different
versions, e.g., E., *Cyclops* 11ff.; Apollodorus 3.5.3; Ovid *Met.* 3.582-691;
Hyginus *Fabulae* 134. In ritual, the arrival of the god was celebrated
from at least the 6th c. on by a procession in which men carried (or
rolled) a ship wreathed with ivy in which sat the god and his priest,
acting as helmsman. The myth in this hymn can be thought of as the
aetion for the ritual, just as the ritual can be seen as an acting out of the
story. Which came first is impossible to tell.

1   On Semele and the story of Dionysos' birth see h. 1.4n.

4-6   The description of Dionysos here is like that of Apollo at h. *Ap.* 450 and
in sharp contrast to the blond, effeminate god of Euripides' *Bacchae.*

approached swiftly over the wine-dark sea,
Tyrsenian pirates,° whom an evil fate was leading. And when they
    saw him
they nodded to each other, leapt out quickly, and at once seized him
and put him on board their ship, rejoicing in their hearts   10
for they thought he was the son of kings cherished by Zeus
And they wanted to tie him with painful bonds
but the bonds did not hold him, and the ropes fell far from
his hands and feet.° And he sat smiling
with his dark-blue eyes. And the helmsman understood   15
and at once called to his comrades and said:

"Fools, what powerful god is this you have taken and bound?
Not even our well-built ship can carry him!
For this is either Zeus or Apollo of the silver bow
or Poseidon since he does not look like mortal   20
men, but like the gods who have their homes on Olympos.
But come, let us release him on the dark mainland
at once! And do not lay your hands on him lest he become angry
and rouse violent winds and a great storm."

So he spoke, but the captain rebuked him with harsh words: 25
"Fool, watch the wind, hoist the ship's sail as soon as
you have gathered all the lines. The men will take care of him.

While Dionysos was represented in Greek art as a young man by the middle of the fifth century (fig. 11), the regular iconography of Dionysos in the archaic period (7th-6th c.) shows an old, bearded figure in a long robe, often wreathed with ivy and carrying a drinking cup.

8   Just who these Tyrsenians were is not clear. At *Th.* 1016 the "very famous Tyrsenians" are said to have been ruled by Agrius and Latinus, whom we know as legendary kings of the early Etruscans. In the *Theogony* these Etruscans evidently lived on remote islands to the northwest of Greece, but the poet gives no further information about them. After Hesiod the name "Tyrsenian" does not reappear in our extant literature (except here) until the fifth century where it is synonymous with "Pelasgian", the name of a pre-Greek people who lived in and around Thrace. Since the Etruscans were well-known in Greek mythology as pirates and since they are clearly the Tyrsenians referred to in Hesiod, it seems reasonable to identify Dionysos' captors with them as well. West (*Th.* 1610 with note) argues that the Greeks would not have been familiar with these Etruscans until around the middle of the sixth century when conflicts between the two peoples first arose. If so, an argument for a sixth century dating of this hymn might be supported.

12-14 This scene is similar to that in the Hermes hymn when Apollo unsuccessfully tries to bind Hermes' hands. The power of the god in each

I suppose he will reach either Egypt or Cyprus or the Hyperboreans°
   or farther away. But in the end
he will tell us at some time about his friends and all his possessions 30
and his brothers, since a god has thrown him to us."

So he spoke and hoisted the mast and sail of the ship.
And a wind blew straight into the sail and they stretched the lines taut
on both sides. But soon wondrous deeds appeared to them.
First of all delicious, sweet-smelling wine trickled along   35
the swift, dark ship, and a divine fragrance
rose up. And astonishment took hold of all the sailors as they
   watched.
Instantly at the very top of the sail a vine spread out
in every direction, and many grapes in clusters
were hanging down. Around the mast dark ivy was
   entwining itself,   40
blooming with flowers, and beautiful berries sprang up°
and all the oarlocks° were wreathed. When they saw
this, only then did the sailors order the helmsman to put the ship
in to shore. But now as they watched, the god became a terrible lion
   in the ship
at the bow and gave a great roar; but now at midship   45

---

   case is demonstrated by the failure of the bonds to hold and underlined
   by the smile of the deity. See h. *H*. 409n.

29 The Hyperboreans were legendary followers of Apollo who lived a life
   of eternal bliss in the far north (their name may mean "those beyond the
   North wind"). They do not appear in Homer, but were known to Hesiod
   (fr. 209), Alcaeus, and Pindar (*O*. 3). Here they are symbolic merely of
   the farthest location the captain can think of as he speaks.

38-41 Other versions of the story describe a variety of "wondrous deeds," e.g.,
   ivy tangling the oars and creeping up the mast (Ovid), or mast and oars
   turning into snakes while the ship fills with ivy (Apollodorus). A
   famous vase-painting by Exekias on the interior of a wine-cup (fig. 11)
   portrays Dionysos (in his archaic form as an older man) reclining in the
   transformed ship, surrounded by dolphins. We can hardly be blamed
   for seeing in it a reflection of this very hymn, although it more likely
   represents a scene from the Dionysos cult (e.g. the ritual ship
   procession), with the dolphins representing the sea rather than the
   transformed pirates.

42 The modern-day oarlock is a U-shaped piece of metal fixed in the
   gunwale (top edge of the ship's side) to hold the oar in place while the
   rower rows. The Greek text actually refers to "thole-pins," the ancient
   equivalent of oarlocks. These were wooden hooks to which each oar
   was attached with a leather loop so it wouldn't slide while in use.

he created a shaggy bear as he showed forth omens.°
And it reared up raging and the lion, on the prow
stood with a terrible glare. The sailors fled to the stern in fear
and stood panic-stricken around the helmsman, who had
a sensible mind. But suddenly the lion sprang   50
and seized the captain and, when they saw this, out they
all leapt at once into the shining sea escaping an evil fate,
and were turned into dolphins. But taking pity on the helmsman,
Dionysos restrained him and made him truly blessed as he said,
"Have courage, ...,° you have delighted my heart.   55
I am loud-roaring Dionysos whom my mother bore,
Kadmos' daughter, Semele, who mingled in love with Zeus "
      Hail, child of fair-faced Semele. There is no way
for the poet who forgets you to compose sweet song.°

8. HYMN TO ARES

Ares, exceedingly mighty, rider of chariots, golden-helmeted,
strong-spirited, shield-carrier, guardian of cities, armed in bronze,
strong-handed, untiring spear-bearer, defender of Olympos,
father of Victory,° successful in war, ally of Themis,

---

46   The Greek word for omen here also signifies the token by which one's
      identity can be confirmed. In this case the ivy, vines, and wild animals
      are all tokens of Dionysos' identity, as well as proof of his power.
55   The surviving text at this point makes no sense, although it may
      contain a corruption of the helmsman's name: "noble Aktor."
59   A very similar ending formula appears at h. 1.18-19, also to Dionysos.
HYMN TO ARES   This hymn is plainly later than the others in the group
      and so unlike them that no one is sure how it came to be placed in the
      Homeric corpus at all. (See introduction on the transmission of the
      hymns in general.) Two characteristics in particular distinguish this
      poem from the rest: the accumulation of the god's epithets (a common
      feature of late hymns), and the focus on Ares not only in his mythical
      aspect as a war god, but also as the planet Mars. The personal nature
      of the poet's prayer in the second half of the hymn also sets it apart
      from the others. Convincing arguments have been made to identify
      Proclus (5th c. AD) as the author of the hymn (cf. M.L. West, CQ 20
      [1970] 300-304).
4   Victory (Nikê) is the daughter of Styx and Pallas in Th. 383-384 and
      Apollodorus 1.2.4. Here the war god Ares is not literally her father, but
      is symbolically linked to Victory, as also to Themis ("Right", on whom
      see h. Ap. 93n.). See below on line 5.

a ruler for enemies, leader of truly just men,°   5
staff-bearer of men's prowess, you who spin your fire-bright sphere
among the planets with their seven paths in the sky, where your fiery
colts ever keep you above the third orbit.°
Hear me, defender of mortals, giver of flourishing youth,
shining down a gentle light from above on my life   10
and my strength in war, so that I may be able
to ward off bitter cowardice from my head,
and to bend the deceptive impulse of my soul with my wits
and to restrain the sharp fury of my heart which provokes me
to enter the icy-cold din of battle. But you, blessed one,   15
grant me courage to stay within the carefree bounds of peace
while escaping the conflict of enemies and violent death.

---

5   To readers of Homer, who portrays an Ares not even his own father
      can love (*Il.* 5.888-898), this connection between Ares and justice or just
      men seems odd. In Homer and other Greek authors, Ares represents
      the painful, hate-filled, evil side of war, while Athena is linked to the
      strength and skill of warriors, the justice of their cause and, ultimately,
      the joy of victory. In this hymn she plays no part at all, while Ares
      assumes her more positive traditional role.

6-8   In these lines the poet addresses the planet Mars. Since adjectives
      formed from the root for "fire" (*pyr-*) are used in astronomical
      literature to describe the characteristic redness of Mars, the epithets
      "fire-bright" and "fiery" in these lines have also been taken to allude
      to the planet's red hue. According to the image here, the planet is
      drawn along its orbit by horses like those of Helios (cf. h. 31.14).
      Among the heavenly signs visible to an ancient astronomer were stars
      which appeared to be fixed in the sky, and seven objects which
      appeared to wander. The seven "wanderers", or *planetes,* had their
      own distinct orbits (or "zones"), and were identified (counting from
      the one closest to the earth) as the moon, the sun, Mercury, Venus,
      Mars, Jupiter, Saturn. While the precise order of the planets varied in
      the observations of different astronomers, the position of Mars was
      always set in the third orbit (counting from the outside).

9. HYMN TO ARTEMIS

Sing, Muse, of Artemis, sister of the far-shooter,
the virgin pourer of arrows, raised together with Apollo.°
She waters her horses at Meles,° deep grown with rushes;
swiftly through Smyrna she drives her golden chariot
to Klaros,° rich in vines, where silver-bowed Apollo   5
sits waiting for the far-shooting pourer of arrows.

And so farewell to you and at the same time to all goddesses
    in my song.°
But you I sing first and with you I begin,
and having begun with you, I will turn to another song.

HYMN TO ARTEMIS   No evidence exists for the date of this hymn. If the references to Artemis' drive from Meles to Smyrna to Klaros (lines 3-5) are taken as aetiological, the hymn may have been composed for a festival at Klaros during which a statue of the goddess was carried from one site to the next in a procession.

2   For these common epithets of Apollo and Artemis, and the story of their birth, see on h. *Ap.* 1, 15 and 16. The goddess is shown shooting her arrows in fig. 2.

3   Meles was a river near the city of Smyrna in Asia Minor, along whose banks Homer was said to have been born (e.g. Moschus 3.70-5) and to have composed his poems in a nearby grotto (Pausanias 7.5.12). According to Quintus Smyrnaeus (7.310) there was a temple to Artemis at Smyrna.

5   Klaros, also in Asia Minor, was the site of both an oracle and a temple of Apollo. See Map 1.

7   This formula appears also at h. 14.6.

10. HYMN TO APHRODITE

Of Cyprus-born Kytherea,° I shall sing, who gives
gentle gifts to mortals, and on her lovely face
always there are smiles and a delightful bloom shines over it.

Farewell, goddess, ruler of well-built Salamis°
and Cyprus on the sea; grant me a delightful song.   5
And I shall remember both you and another song.

11. HYMN TO ATHENA

Pallas Athena, defender of cities,° I begin to sing,
awesome one, who, along with Ares,° cares for deeds of war
and the sacking of cities and the battle-cry and wars,
and she saves the people as they go out and return.

Farewell, goddess; grant me good fortune and joy.   5

HYMN TO APHRODITE
1   On the epithets "Cyprus-born," and "Kytherea" see the introduction to
        h. *Aph.*, h. *Aph.* 2n., and 6n.
4   Salamis was the main city on the island of Cyprus.
HYMN TO ATHENA
1   Athena is called "defender of cities" also at *Il.* 6.305 but, as a goddess
        of war, she is also the destroyer of cities as in line 3 of this hymn. This
        endowing of a god or goddess with contrary powers (e.g. of both
        protection and destruction) was characteristic of the Greeks. Thus
        Athena both protects warriors (4) and causes their death in war,
        Hermes is the patron of thieves who also guards the house (h. *H.* 15n.),
        and Artemis is the huntress who also watches over the birth of wild
        animals.
2   Athena and Ares rarely appear together in myth or ritual, although
        Pindar (*N.* 10.84) links the two as deities of war, and Pausanias reports
        two instances of their connection in sanctuaries at Olympia (5.15.6)
        and Athens (1.8.4). Ares appears (with Hermes, Apollo, and Eileithyia)
        at the birth of Athena on a black-figure amphora of the 6th century BC
        (fig. 4).

12. HYMN TO HERA

Hera I sing, the golden-throned one whom Rhea bore,
queen of the immortals, beautiful beyond all others,
sister of loud-thundering Zeus and glorious
wife, whom all the blessed ones throughout lofty Olympos
honor, reverencing her equally with Zeus who delights in thunder.   5

13. HYMN TO DEMETER

Fair-haired Demeter, holy goddess, I begin to sing,
her and her daughter, very beautiful Persephone.

Farewell, goddess, stand by this city, and begin my song.

HYMN TO HERA   This hymn, unlike any other in the corpus (except h. 8
    which is much later than the rest), lacks any farewell formula.
    Whether this is an accident of transmission, or the lines which remain
    were once part of a longer hymn, is unknown.
HYMN TO DEMETER   The shortest "hymn" in the corpus, this poem is
    merely a combination of formulae from other songs: line 1 = h. *Dem.* 1,
    line 2 = h. *Dem.* 493 (modified so the goddess and her daughter
    become the object rather than the subject of the verse), and line 3 (up
    to "city") recurs in Callimachus' *Hymn to Demeter* 134. It provides,
    nonetheless, a good example of the standard greeting and farewell
    patterns in the hymns.

14. HYMN TO THE MOTHER
OF THE GODS

Sing to me, Muse, clear-voiced daughter of great Zeus,
about the Mother of all gods and of all men,
to whom the sound of castanets and drums along with the piercing
    sound of flutes°
is a delight, and the howling of wolves and flashing-eyed lions,°
and echoing mountains and wooded glens.   5

And so farewell to you and at the same time to all goddesses in my
    song.

HYMN TO THE MOTHER OF THE GODS   Archaeological discoveries
from the Early Neolithic period at Çatal Hüyük reveal wall paintings
and a statuette of a female figure, flanked by animals, giving birth that
provides a striking parallel to the Great Mother goddess known in
Asia Minor by the seventh century BC as Kybele. One Linear B tablet
from Pylos (Fr 1202) also documents offerings to a Divine Mother. For
the later Greeks this "Mother of the Gods" was usually associated in
myth with Rhea (sometimes also with Demeter) and was worshipped
in cult, more in private rites than public, simply as Mother. Herodotus
4.76 provides the first extant literary reference to her. We have no clear
evidence for the date of this hymn in which the goddess is not named.
3   The worship of Kybele is also traditionally associated with orgiastic
rites accompanied by the sound of drums, cymbals, and flutes. The
ancient "flute" (aulos) was actually a kind of reed-pipe which may
have sounded more like an oboe than a modern flute and which was
often played by women (in contrast to the lyre played by men).
4   Lions (and other wild animals) are often shown in representations of
the divine mother figure, perhaps as a symbol of her fertility. Cf. also
h. *Aph.* 70.

15. HYMN TO HERAKLES THE LION-HEARTED

Herakles, son of Zeus, I will sing, by far the greatest
of men, whom Alkmene bore in Thebes, city of beautiful dances,
after she mingled in love with the dark-clouded son of Kronos.°
Before, wandering over endless earth and sea
on missions for lord Eurystheus,°   5
he performed many reckless deeds himself and suffered many things.

HYMN TO HERAKLES THE LION-HEARTED   This hymn to Herakles
probably dates to the 6th century BC or later, since Greek myth does not
treat Herakles as a god before then (see 5n.), but there is no evidence on
which to assign it a place of origin. The epithet "lion-hearted"
(*leontothumon*) is not known elsewhere, although Hesychius preserves
the similar compound *thumoleonta*.

3   The story of Herakles' birth was told in many sources, including the
Hesiodic *Shield of Herakles* (ca. 7th c. B.C.), Pi *N*. 1, Apollodorus, lost plays
of both Sophocles and Euripides, and Plautus' comedy, the *Amphitruo*.
According to the Hesiodic account, Alkmene's husband, Amphitryon,
had sworn an oath not to make love with her until he had avenged the
deaths of her brothers. While he was performing this task, Zeus went to
Alkmene disguised as her husband, and slept with her. The real
Amphitryon returned on the same night and also slept with his wife. As a
result, Alkmene bore twin sons, Herakles, the son of Zeus, and Iphicles,
the son of Amphitryon. A common variation of this version has Zeus
extending the length of his one night with Alkmene by persuading the
sun not to rise for three days. For other twin sons of an immortal and a
mortal father, cf. Kastor and Polydeukes (see h. 33 with notes).
        The origins of Herakles remain uncertain, although there is good
evidence to connect him with figures of eastern myth. Whatever his
origins, however, Herakles became the greatest hero of the Greeks and,
after completing his many forced labors, he was ultimately granted status
as a god. His name at least appears to carry an explicit connection with
the goddess Hera combining her name, *Hera*, with the word kleos, "fame,
glory," to suggest that his fame came about through her (see 5n. below).

5   Eurystheus was king of Tiryns and a cousin of Herakles who gained
authority over that hero through a trick of Hera's. The *Iliad* (19.96-132)

But now in a beautiful home on snowy Olympos
he lives in joy and has fair-ankled Hebe as his wife.°

Farewell, lord, son of Zeus, and grant me excellence and happiness.°

16. HYMN TO ASKLEPIOS

Healer of illnesses, Asklepios, begin to sing,
the son of Apollo whom noble Koronis
daughter of king Phlegyas bore on the plain of Dotion,°

records how Zeus once boasted that a descendant of his blood would be born that day who would rule over all those living near him. Knowing that he referred to Herakles, but determined to deceive her husband, Hera tricked Zeus into swearing an oath to confirm his boast. She then delayed the birth of Herakles, and contrived the premature birth of Eurystheus in his mother's seventh month of pregnancy.

Hera's hatred of Herakles is a constant theme in the cycle of myths surrounding him. After sending snakes to kill him as a baby, Hera imposed on Herakles a madness which caused him to kill his first wife (Megara) and their three children. After seeking purification for this act, he went to Delphi to seek the advice of the oracle. There, for the first time, he was called *Hera-kleos*, and was told that if he served Eurystheus for twelve years, he would be given immortality. This last part of the myth, the deification of Herakles, seems to be a later addition to the cycle of stories surrounding him, and cannot be dated before the 6th century BC given our extant sources.

8   Hebe, the goddess of youth, was one of three children born to Zeus and Hera (the others were Ares, god of war, and Eileithyia, goddess of childbirth). After Herakles was granted immortality and reconciled with Hera, he was given Hebe, the personification of eternal youth, for his wife.

9   The final phrase here is formulaic and conventional, but its precise meaning is open to interpretation. The god is asked to grant *arete* and *olbos*. *Arete* can mean "excellence," "virtue" and, in some instances, even "success." *Olbos* may mean "happiness" and "wealth" or "prosperity".

HYMN TO ASKLEPIOS   There is no evidence on which to base a reliable date or place of composition for this hymn. Asklepios, "the blameless physician", is mentioned in the *Iliad* (11.518) as the king of Trikke in Thessaly (see Map 2), and as the father of two sons, Machaon and Podaleirios, who are both also physicians (2.732). Although originally a mortal, Asklepios came to be worshipped as a god, with a cult first (apparently) at Trikke, and in Hellenistic times at Epidauros and Kos.

3   Hesiod fr. 58, Pindar *P*.3, and Ovid *Met*. 2.600-634 all give versions of the story of Asklepios' birth to Koronis and Apollo: already pregnant with

a great joy to mortals and a soother of evil pains.

And so fairwell to you, lord; I pray to you in my song.   5

---

17. HYMN TO THE DIOSKOUROI

Sing, clear-voiced Muse, of Kastor and Polydeukes
the Tyndaridai who were born from Olympian Zeus
Beneath the peak of Taygetos queenly Leda bore them
having yielded in secret to the dark-clouded son of Kronos.

Farewell, Tyndaridai, riders of swift horses.   5

---

18. HYMN TO HERMES

Hermes, I sing, the Kyllenian Argeiphontes
ruler of Kyllene and Arkadia, rich in flocks,
swift messenger of the immortals, whom Maia bore,
the reverent daughter of Atlas, mingling in love with Zeus.
But she avoided the company of the blessed gods,   5
living in a shady cave where the son of Kronos
used to mingle in love with the fair-haired nymph in the dark of
    night,

Asklepios, Koronis made love with a mortal and was killed by Apollo himself, or by Artemis at the behest of Apollo. The god, taking pity on his unborn son, snatched him from the dying Koronis' womb and handed him over to the centaur Chiron to be raised and taught the art of medicine. Asklepios himself is later killed by Zeus for bringing a dead man back to life (Pi. P.3.54-58).

HYMN TO THE DIOSKOUROI   Like h. 18 to Hermes, this hymn seems to be an abbreviation of the longer hymn to the Dioskouroi (h. 33), although it lacks the final promise of the singer to sing another song. See notes on h. 33.

HYMN TO HERMES   This hymn appears to be an abstract of the longer h. H., but there is no evidence for its date. Lines 1-7 are almost identical to those in h. H. — see notes there.

unnoticed by both immortal gods and mortal men,
while sweet sleep held white-armed Hera

And so farewell to you, son of Zeus and Maia.   10
But having begun with you, I will turn to another song.
Farewell, Hermes giver of joy, guide, giver of blessings.

19. HYMN TO PAN

About the dear son of Hermes, Muse, sing to me,
the goat-footed, two-horned lover of noise, who roams
through tree-filled meadows in the company of dancing nymphs.
They tread down the peaks of sheer° rock
calling on Pan the shepherd god, unwashed,   5
with splendid hair, who has as his lot every snowy hill-crest
and the peaks of mountains and rocky paths.
He wanders here and there through thick brushwood,
now drawn by gentle streams,
now again he wanders on towering cliffs,   10
and climbs up to the highest peak overlooking the flocks.
Often he runs through tall, white mountains,
often he hunts wild beasts on the mountain slopes, killing them,
as he keeps a sharp watch. But then only at evening he sounds a shrill
    cry
as he returns from the chase playing a sweet tune   15
on his reed-pipes.° Nor could that bird surpass him in song

HYMN TO PAN The hymn to Pan is later than most of the other hymns in
    the corpus, and probably dates to 500-450 BC, but almost certainly
    after the Hymn to Hermes, whose influence (from lines 2-4) can be
    seen in lines 28-34 of this hymn. The cult of Pan centered in Arkadia
    but, according to Herodotus (6.105), the god was worshipped in
    Athens after the battle of Marathon in 490 BC. There is not enough
    evidence to prove an Athenian origin for the hymn, however.
4   The adjective here means literally that the rocks are so steep as to be
    "deserted by goats" (except, of course by the goat-footed god).
16 As a rustic god, Pan is often associated with the simple reed pipes
    (*syrinx*) used by shepherds in ancient Greece. Ovid (*Met.* 1.689-712)
    tells how Pan once pursued the nymph Syrinx, who turned into a bed
    of marsh reeds as she fled his advances. When the god heard the
    beautiful sound of the wind blowing through these reeds, he cut two
    of them and made the reed pipe which was associated with him from
    that point on. Another version of the pipes' invention is given in h. *H.*
    511-512, where Hermes invents the instrument after giving up the lyre
    to Apollo.

which utters a honey-voiced melody as she pours forth her lament°
amid the leaves of flower-laden spring.
With him then the clear-voiced mountain nymphs,
moving on nimble feet, sing by a spring of dark water   20
and the echo sounds around the mountain-peak.
The god moving on this side of the chorus and that, and then into the
    middle,
directs the dance with his quick feet. On his back he wears
the tawny hide of a lynx, as he delights his heart with clear songs
in a soft meadow where crocus and sweet-smelling hyacinth   25
bloom, mixed in at random in the grass.
They sing the blessed gods and high Olympos
and they sing of swift Hermes above the rest,
how he is the swift messenger of all the gods
and how he came to Arkadia with her many springs,
    mother of flocks,   30
where there is a sacred precinct for him as god of Kyllene
There, although he was a god, he tended rough-haired sheep
for a mortal man. For a soft desire came upon him and grew strong
to mingle in love with the fair-haired nymph, the daughter of Dryops.
And he brought to pass a fruitful marriage and soon after, in the
    house,   35
Dryope bore to Hermes a dear son, a marvel to look at,
with goat's feet and two horns, boisterous and laughing sweetly.
But his mother leapt up and fled, leaving the child,
for she was afraid when she saw his harsh appearance and full
    beard.
But swift Hermes at once picked him up and took him in his arms,   40
and the god rejoiced beyond measure in his heart.
He wrapped the child in the thick skins of a mountain hare
and went quickly to the homes of the immortals.
And he set him before Zeus and the other immortals,
and showed them his boy. And all the immortals   45
were delighted in their hearts, but above all Bacchic Dionysos.
And they called him Pan because he delighted the hearts of all.°

And so farewell to you, lord; I seek your favor with my song.
And I will remember you and another song.

---

17   The nightingale.
47   The Greek word *pan* means "all".

20. HYMN TO HEPHAISTOS

Sing, clear-voiced Muse, of Hephaistos, famed for his inventiveness,
who along with grey-eyed Athena taught glorious crafts°
to men on the earth, who formerly
used to live in caves on the mountains like wild animals.
But now, because of Hephaistos, famed for his skill, having learned
  crafts,   5
they easily lead their lives for the full year
free from care in their own houses.

But be propitious, Hephaistos, and grant me excellence and happiness.°

HYMN TO HEPHAISTOS   Hephaistos was originally a non-Greek god,
  whose name seems to appear on a Linear B tablet at Knossos (KN L
  588). His primary cult was located on the island of Lemnos, but he was
  worshipped in Athens as well, with a large temple, the *Hephaistion*,
  dedicated to him in the second half of the fifth century. That
  Hephaistos and Athena shared a cult in Athens is attested both by the
  statue of Athena which stood in the *Hephaistion*, and the smiths'
  festival, *Chalkeia*, which honored the two gods together. The shared
  cult at Athens, however, is not sufficient evidence for an Attic origin of
  the hymn.
2   The word for "crafts" here (and in line 5) is *erga*, a word often
  translated "works". Athena, herself called *Ergane*, "Worker," and
  Hephaistos, the god of fire and the divine smith associated with skill
  and art (*techne*), were known as patrons of civilization both by Plato
  (*Laws* 920d, *Protag.* 321d, etc.) and, later, in the Orphic religion (*Orph.*
  fr. 178, 179). For Hephaistos and Athena as teachers of craft elsewhere,
  cf. Od. 6.232-234, and *WD* 59-64.
8   Cf. h. 15.9n for the final formula.

21. HYMN TO APOLLO

Phoibos, even the swan sings of you in a clear tone to the beat of her wings°
as she alights on the bank along the eddying river
Peneios.° And you the sweet-voiced singer
with his clear-toned lyre always sings first and last.

And so farewell to you, lord; I seek your favor with my song.   5

22. HYMN TO POSEIDON

Of Poseidon, the great god, I begin to sing,
shaker of the earth and of the barren sea,
god of the sea who holds Helikon and wide Aigai.°
A double honor did the gods allot to you, Earthshaker,

HYMN TO APOLLO   We have no evidence for the date or place of composition of this hymn.
1   For the song of the bird blended with the sound of its wings, cf. Aristophanes, *Birds* 771.
3   The Peneios was a river in Thessaly.
HYMN TO POSEIDON
3   The cities of Helike (on the Gulf of Corinth) and Aigai (located, variously, on the Gulf of Corinth or in Thrace), were sacred to Poseidon in antiquity (cf. *Il.* 2.575, 8.203, 13.21, *Od.* 5.381), but the text here seems firm in naming Mt. Helikon (in Boiotia, see Map 2), where no cult of Poseidon was known. The god is called *Helikonios* at *Il.* 20.404, and was worshipped under the cult title *Helikonios* on Mt. Mykale in Asia Minor (Hdt. 1.148), but it is linguistically impossible to link that title with the name Helike. It is hard to be certain whether Helikon or Helike was intended by the hymnist, who may himself have been confused.

to be both tamer of horses and savior of ships.° 5

Farewell, Poseidon, dark-haired holder of the earth,
and, blessed one, with a kindly heart help those on the sea.

23. HYMN TO ZEUS

Zeus I will sing, the best and greatest of the gods,
far-seeing, all powerful lord who whispers
his secret schemes to Themis as she sits leaning towards him.

Be propitious, far-seeing son of Kronos, most glorious and greatest.

24. HYMN TO HESTIA

Hestia, you who tend the sacred house
of lord Apollo the far-shooter, in holy Pytho,°
from your locks moist olive oil always trickles down.°

---

5   Cf. also Paus. 7.21.9. Poseidon is known as a horse tamer already in the
        Iliad (23.307), and was regularly associated with horses in cult. He was
        worshipped by the Greeks as the savior of men at sea after a storm in
        480 BC which damaged the Persian fleet near Thessaly. He appears
        with his regular attributes, a trident and a small dolphin, on a black
        figure amphora from the end of the 6th-century BC (fig. 3).
HYMN TO ZEUS
5   The Titan Themis was Zeus' second wife (*Th.* 901-906). Her name
        means "right, custom".
HYMN TO HESTIA   Hestia, whose name means "hearth", is goddess of the
        hearth and the hearth fire, who was rarely personified in Greek myth
        or art. The reference to Delphi in lines 1-2 does not necessarily prove a
        Delphic origin for this hymn, since the sacred hearth at that site was
        considered the central point of the world and the source of sacred fire
        for all Greek cities.
2   Pytho = Delphi See h. *Ap.* 374n.
3   This line likely refers to the practice in antiquity of mixing olive oil
        with herbs or spices to use as perfume. Perfumed oil was poured on
        sacred statues and stones as well.

Come to this house. Come, keeping your spirit
aligned with Zeus the contriver.° And grant favor to my song.   5

25. HYMN TO THE MUSES AND APOLLO

From the Muse let me begin and from Apollo and Zeus,
For it is through the Muses and far-shooting Apollo
that there are singers and lyre-players upon the earth,
but kings are from Zeus. And blessed is the one whom the Muses
love, for sweet speech flows from his mouth.   5

Farewell, children of Zeus, and honor my song.
And I will remember you and another song too.

26. HYMN TO DIONYSOS

Ivy-crowned Dionysos of the loud cry I begin to sing,
splendid son of Zeus and glorious Semele,
whom the fair-haired nymphs received from the lord, his father,
and nourished at their breasts and raised tenderly

4-5   The invocation of Zeus along with Hestia here may suggest the
        dedication of a temple, rather than an occasion in a private home.
HYMN TO THE MUSES AND APOLLO   This hymn appears to be an
        abstract from Hesiod with lines 2-5 virtually identical to *Th.* 94-97, and
        lines 1 and 6 modelled on *Th.* 1 and 104, respectively. The date of the
        hymn can, therefore, be fixed after that of Hesiod.
2   The connection of the Muses and Apollo as lovers and patrons of
        music is commonplace, cf. *Il.* 1.601-604, h. *Ap.* 189, h. *H.* 450. See Fig. 8.
HYMN TO DIONYSOS   There is no evidence for the date or place of
        composition of this hymn, although it is easy to imagine it being sung
        at a festival to Dionysos. For notes on Semele and Nysa, see h. 1.4n.
        and 8n.

in the hollows of Nysa. And he grew by the grace of his father   5
in a fragrant cave, counted among the immortals.
But when indeed the goddesses had raised him with many songs,
then indeed he started to roam the wooded glens,
decked with ivy and laurel. The nymphs followed
him, but he led, and their cries filled the boundless forest.   10

And so farewell to you, Dionysos, rich in grapes.
Grant that we may come rejoicing again next year,
and from then again for many years.

27. HYMN TO ARTEMIS

Loud-crying Artemis of the golden bow I sing,
the reverent maiden, rainer of arrows,° who strikes deer,
twin sister of Apollo of the golden sword,°
she who, through shady mountains and wind-swept hill-tops,
delighting in the hunt, stretches her golden bow   5
as she sends forth her painful shafts. The peaks of lofty
mountains tremble, and the thick-shaded forest echoes
dreadfully with the cries of wild animals, and the earth shudders
and the fishy sea. But she, with a stout heart,
turns in all directions as she slays the race of wild animals.   10

But when the arrow-pouring huntress has taken her pleasure
and delighted her heart, she unstrings her well-crafted bow,
and goes to the great house of her dear brother
Phoibos Apollo, to the rich district of Delphi,
to prepare the beautiful dance of the Muses and Graces.   15
There she hangs her curved bow and arrows
and, wearing her lovely jewelry, she is their leader
as she begins the dance. And they send forth a divine voice
as they sing how fair-ankled Leto bore children
by far the best of the immortals in both counsel and deeds.   20

Farewell, children of Zeus and fair-haired Leto.
And I will remember you and another song too.

HYMN TO ARTEMIS   This hymn shows the influence of the longer Hymn to
      Apollo, with particular similarities to the Delian portion. Its date may be
      ca. 585 BC.
2   For Artemis' epithet see h. *Ap.* 15n.
3   For Apollo's connection with the sword, see h. *Ap.* 123n.
19   See h. *Ap.* 5n.

28. HYMN TO ATHENA

Pallas Athena, glorious goddess, I begin to sing,
grey-eyed, resourceful, with an unyielding heart,
the reverent maiden, mighty defender of cities,
Tritogeneia,° whom Zeus the deviser himself bore
from his august head, wearing weapons of war   5
shining, golden. And awe held all the immortals
who saw her. Before Zeus the aegis bearer°
she sprang quickly out of his immortal head,
brandishing a sharp spear. Great Olympos was shaken
dreadfully by the fearful strength of the grey-eyed goddess,
          and the earth   10
all around echoed awesomely, and the sea was moved
and churned up with storm-dark waves. Then the sea-water held back

---

HYMN TO ATHENA   The date and origin of this hymn are unknown, but its
     style, like that of h. 27 to Artemis, suggests that its author was
     influenced by the *Hymn to Apollo*. The story of Athena's birth is told by
     Hesiod (*Th.* 886-900, 924-926), who says Zeus swallowed the pregnant
     goddess Metis and later gave birth to Athena out of his head. This hymn
     emphasizes Athena's appearance in full armor (lines 5-6, 15), a detail not
     mentioned in Hesiod, but apparently contained in a lost work by the
     lyric poet Stesichoros (ca. 7th-6th c. BC), and a common theme in vase
     painting from the 6th-century BC on (see fig. 4).
4   The title, *Tritogeneia,* which appears in Homer, Hesiod, and later authors,
     was used only of Athena, but its origin and meaning are unknown. The
     second part of the word (*geneia*) refers to birth, but the sense of the first part
     has been disputed. The best guess may be that it means "true-born",
     "genuine daughter", referring to Athena's legitimacy as the motherless
     child born from Zeus' head. Less convincing theories are 1) that it refers to a
     myth in which Zeus gave his newborn daughter to the river god Triton (in
     Boiotia or Thessaly) or the lake god Tritonis (in Libya) to raise, although we
     know of no other connection between this goddess and water, or 2) if *trito*
     means "third", that it refers either to her place as Zeus' third-born child
     (after Artemis and Apollo), or to her birth on the third day of the month.
7   On Zeus' aegis see. h. *H.* 183n.

suddenly,° and the glorious son of Hyperion stood
his swift-footed horses long enough for the maiden,
Pallas Athena, to take the divine weapons   15
from her immortal shoulders. And Zeus the deviser laughed.

And so farewell to you, child of aegis-bearing Zeus,
And I will remember you and another song too.

29. HYMN TO HESTIA

Hestia, in the lofty homes of all,
both of immortal gods and of men who walk the earth,
you have won as your lot an eternal seat and the highest honor,
possessing a noble prize and portion of honor — for without you
there are no banquets for mortals where they do not begin
    by pouring   5
libations of sweet-smelling wine to Hestia first and last° —
and you, Argeiphontes, son of Zeus and Maia,
messenger of the blessed gods, god with the golden staff, giver of
    blessings,
dwell in this noble house, dear to one another's hearts°
. . . .
being propitious, come to our aid with the reverent and friendly   10
Hestia. For, since you both know the noble deeds
of men on earth, follow them with counsel and strength.

Farewell, daughter of Kronos and you too, Hermes with the golden

12-13 Athena's appearance first disturbs all nature, then brings its course
    momentarily to a stop. Thus the heaving of the sea stops, and the sun,
    Hyperion, stops his chariot in its journey across the sky. Pi O.7.38
    describes a similar shivering of the earth and sky at Athena's birth.
HYMN TO HESTIA   We have no special evidence for the date or place of
    origin of this hymn, which seems to honor Hermes (Argeiphontes) as
    much as Hestia These two gods were closely associated with mortals
    as protectors of the home and bringers of good luck, and their
    appearance together in this hymn may argue for its performance at a
    private house.
6   There is a lot of evidence that Hestia did receive the first libation (cf.
    the opening prayer to Hestia at Pi . N. 11.1-7), while Hermes conven-
    tionally received the last libation after an evening feast (Od. 7.137-138).
    One ancient source (Cornutus 53) explains that Hestia received the
    first and last libation because she was both the first swallowed and the
    last regurgitated by Kronos.
9   There appears to be a loss of at least one line after l. 9.

162

staff.
And I will remember you and another song too.

30. HYMN TO EARTH, MOTHER OF ALL

Deep-rooted Earth I shall sing, mother of all,
and oldest, who nourishes all that exists on the earth,
whatever goes upon the shining land, whatever moves in the sea,
whatever flies, all these are nourished by your bounty.
From you, queen, men are blessed with children and good   5
harvests, from you comes the power to grant life to mortal men, and
to take it away. He is blessed whom you honor
willingly in your heart; all things are his in abundance.
His life-giving fields are laden with fruit, his pastures
flourish with flocks and herds, and his house is full of riches.   10
Men such as these rule with good laws in the cities
of beautiful women, and much happiness and wealth attend them.
Their sons glory in youthful merriment,
and their daughters, with joyful heart, play
in flower-laden choruses and skip over the soft flowers of the field.   15
These are the men you honor, holy goddess, bountiful deity.

Farewell, mother of the gods, wife of starry Ouranos
and for my song, kindly grant delightful sustenance.
And I will remember you and another song too.

HYMN TO EARTH, MOTHER OF ALL   This hymn has been compared to
Orphic hymn 26, which also honors Gaia, but there is no evidence
either for its date or for the occasion of its performance. The style of
the hymn to Earth and of the next two hymns (to Helios and Selene) is
similar, and seems to place them outside the mainstream of the other
hymns. As in Hesiod's *Theogony*, the earth here is seen as the
primordial mother of all, but there is no indication of whether or not
the poet sees her in a personified form.

31. HYMN TO HELIOS

Begin to sing again, O Muse Kalliope,° daughter of Zeus,
about Helios the radiant god, whom cow-eyed Euryphaëssa°
bore to the son of Gaia and starry Ouranos.
For Hyperion° married the famous Euryphaëssa,
his own sister, who bore him beautiful children,   5
Eos of the rosyarms and fair-haired Selene,
and tireless Helios like the immortals,°
who shines on mortals and immortal gods
as he drives his horses. With his eyes he flashes a piercing look
from his golden helmet, and bright beams shine radiantly   10
from him, while from his head and over his temples
the bright cheekpieces cover his graceful face
shining from afar. On his skin a beautiful, finely-woven garment
shimmers in the blast of the winds, and his stallions

. . . .

HYMN TO HELIOS   This hymn, like the next to Selene, evidently served as a
    prelude to an epic recitation, for the singer promises to "celebrate the
    race of mortal men," rather than to move on to praise another god. Both
    hymns share similar language and style, and may have been composed
    by the same hymnist. Helios was not an important figure in cult, except
    at Rhodes and, perhaps, at an early stage in the Peloponnese. For other
    hymns to Helios, cf. Orphic hymn 8 and Proclus h. 1.
1   Kalliope is named as one of the nine muses in Hesiod (*Th.* 79) and is
    mentioned also in Alcman fr. 27 (PMG). In later tradition she was
    identified as the patroness of epic poetry.
2   The name Euryphaëssa, which means "Widely-shining," appears only
    here, perhaps as another name for Theia, the mother of Helios (Sun),
    Selene (Moon), and Eos (Dawn) in Hesiod (*Th.* 371-374); see
    genealogical chart.
4   Hyperion is a Titan whose major significance is as the father of Helios.
    Like Helios, Hyperion too is a sun god. For similar redundancy of
    function among the Greek pantheon, cf. Ouranos and Zeus as gods of
    the sky, and the three generations of sea gods (Pontos, Okeanos, and
    Poseidon).
7   This line echoes *Il.* 11.60, so the epithet "like the immortals" need not be
    taken to imply that Helios was inferior to the other gods.

He stays his golden-yoked chariot and horses there   15
until he sends them wondrously through the heavens to the ocean.°

Farewell, lord, kindly grant delightful sustenance.
Having begun from you I will celebrate the race of mortal men,
the demigods whose deeds the gods have shown to men.

32. HYMN TO SELENE

Muses skilled in song, sweet-voiced daughters of Zeus,
son of Kronos, sing next of long-winged Moon.°
From her immortal head a radiance appearing from heaven
swirls to the earth, and great beauty rises up slowly
from the shining radiance. The air, unlit before, glistens   5
with light from her golden crown, and her beams linger in the air
whenever divine Selene, after she bathes her beautiful skin
in the Ocean, puts on her far-shining robes,
and yokes her strong-necked, glistening colts,
drives forth her beautifully-maned horses swiftly   10
in the evening at mid-month. Her great orbit is full
then, and as she waxes her beams become brightest

15-16 For the chariot of Helios cf. h. *Dem.* 63n. Although a line seems to be
       missing before these lines, the sense is clear enough. Helios drives his
       chariot to the mid-point of the sky, where the sun appears to pause
       before beginning its descent to the horizon and, eventually, to the
       ocean. According to the ancients, the sun traveled across the sky from
       east to west during the day and sailed back to the east on the ocean
       during the night. The 7th-century poet Mimnermos (fr. 10) described
       Helios' nightly journey in a golden, winged cup fashioned by
       Hephaistos which carried the god from west to east as he slept.

HYMN TO SELENE   Selene was not an important figure in cult, although
       the moon was, at times, identified with other more prominent
       goddesses (Artemis, Hekate, Persephone). Her place in myth is
       secured primarily by the story of the shepherd boy, Endymion, with
       whom she fell in love as he lay sleeping in a cave on Mt. Latmos
       (Sappho fr. 199 LP). As a result of this love (whether by way of
       punishment or reward), he was granted eternal youth and perpetual
       sleep by Zeus. Orphic hymn 9 is also addressed to the Moon.

2   Selene (Moon) appears nowhere else in art or literature as a winged
       figure, but Eos (Dawn) regularly has wings. Whether the poet
       confused the two, or chose to transfer the image from one sister to the
       other, is uncertain.

in the heavens.° So she is a fixed token and sign to mortals.

Once the son of Kronos mingled in love with her
and she became pregnant and bore a daughter, Pandeia,°   15
who has outstanding beauty among the immortal gods.

Farewell, white-armed goddess, bright Selene
kind lady with the beautiful hair. Having begun with you I shall sing
of the glories of men, the demigods, whose deeds singers,
servants of the Muses, celebrate with their lovely mouths.   20

33. HYMN TO THE DIOSKOUROI

Quick-glancing Muses, sing the sons of Zeus,°

11-13 The ancients measured months according to the waxing and waning of
the moon, so that each month began with the appearance of the new
moon, and mid-month coincided with the full moon. Cf. Pi. *O*. 3.19.

15 Pandeia ("All-shining") seems to be an abstraction of the moon. There
was a festival at mid-month in Athens called Pandia, but it is uncertain
whether any connection existed between it and the figure named here.

HYMN TO DIOSKOUROI A 6th-century BC inscription found at Kephallenia,
and apparently combining a phrase from line 9 of this hymn with one
from *Il*. 2.631, has suggested an early date for this hymn. Scholars have
also noted parallels with *h*. 7 to Dionysos. The origin of the twin
brothers known as the Dioskouroi remains uncertain. They may have
been local heroes elevated to divine status (like Herakles), as the
poems of Homer and Hesiod imply. On the other hand, they may be
examples of "faded" gods, figures worshipped at one time (or in one
culture) as deities, but eventually accepted in myth as mere mortals.
Taking the second view, many scholars have connected the Dioskouroi
with the twin Asvin of Vedic mythology, divine figures who, like the
Dioskouroi, were riders of shining horses and saviors of men.

1 This line provides the first identification of Kastor and Polydeukes as
dios kouroi, literally "sons of Zeus", but the very next line also names
them as *Tyndaridai* "sons of Tyndareus". The story of the two brothers
is complicated, with many different traditions that sometimes overlap
in their details. The *Iliad* knows the tradition that Kastor and
Polydeukes were mortal sons of Tyndareus who died and were buried
in Lakedaimon (Il. 3.236-244). The Odyssey names Leda as their
mother and Tyndareus as their father, yet adds that they are honored
like gods (11.301-304):
>   the life-giving earth holds them both alive
>   and, having honor from Zeus, even below the earth,
>   now they live on alternate days and now again
>   they die. But they have honor equal to the gods.

the Tyndaridai, glorious children of fair-ankled Leda,°
Kastor, the tamer of horses, and blameless Polydeukes.
Beneath the peak of great Mt. Taygetos
she mingled in love with the dark-clouded son of Kronos   5
and bore these children, saviors of men upon the earth,
and of swift ships, when wintry storm blasts
rage over the pitiless sea.° And the men on the ships
call on the sons of great Zeus offering prayers
with white lambs, as they mount the topmost points   10
of the stern. The great wind and waves of the sea
force the ship under water, but suddenly they appear,
darting through the air on steady-beating wings,
and at once they check the blasts of harsh winds,
and smooth the waves on the white-capped sea.   15
For sailors they are fair signs of their toil, and seeing them
they rejoice and stop their painful toil.

Farewell, Tyndaridai, riders of swift horses.°
And I will remember you and another song.

Hesiod (*Ehoiai* 66 Loeb) calls both the sons of Zeus, but Pindar (*N*.10.49-90) preserves the story of how Zeus slept with Leda on the same night as Tyndareus, so that twins were born, one (Kastor) fathered by the mortal Tyndareus, and the other (Polydeukes) fathered by Zeus himself. When the mortal Kastor was killed in a fight, his brother Polydeukes chose to give up his immortality so the two could be together, beneath the earth half the time, and on Olympos the other half. Later tradition alters this scheme so that while one brother lives, the other is dead on alternating days.

2   Leda, the wife of the Spartan king Tyndareus, is famous because of her children. In addition to Kastor and Polydeukes (called Pollux by the Romans), she also bore Klytemnaistra and Helen. The hymn makes no mention of these sisters, or of how Zeus visited Leda in the shape of a swan to father Helen (cf. Euripides, *Helen* 16-22; Lucian, *Dialogues of the Gods* 20). The tradition that the twins also hatched from a swan's egg dates to the Alexandrian period.

4   Mt. Taygetos is located southwest of Sparta in Lakedaimon, where worship of the Dioskouroi in Greece seems to have begun. See Map 2.

8   The Dioskouroi's place as saviors of those in trouble at sea is traditional, and led to their identification with the lights of St. Elmo's fire, the sparks set off from a ship's mast during a thunderstorm.

18   Both twins were connected with horses, often called "riders of white horses" (Pi. *P.* 1.66), although Kastor alone of the two was known as a "tamer of horses" (*Il.* 3.237). This connection with horses is reflected in myth by the story of how the Dioskouroi abducted two daughters of Leukippos ("White Horse"), and in cult by the title *Leukippides*

34. HYMN TO GUEST-FRIENDS

Respect the one who needs your gifts of friendship and a home,
you who dwell in the sheer city of Hera, the lovely-faced nymph,
at the foot of towering Saidene,
drinking the divine water of the golden river
Hermos, flowing beautifully, whom immortal Zeus begat.

("daughters of Leukippos") which was given to their priestesses in
Sparta. Ashvin, the name of the Vedic twins with whom the
Dioskouroi are often connected, means "having horses".
HYMN TO GUEST-FRIENDS   This poem, not itself a hymn, is appended at
the end of the collection of hymns in several, but not all, manuscripts
of the *Homeric Hymns*. It is also included with other "Homeric"
Epigrams preserved in the pseudo-Herodotean *Life of Homer*, which
dates to ca. 200 AD and may be of Aeolic origin. The text of the version
given here differs from that in the *Life of Homer* in several places, but
both versions refer to the area of Kyme and the river Hermos in Aeolis
(see Map 1). How this epigram came to be grouped with the hymns is
unknown.

PRONUNCIATION GUIDE

In the guide that follows, syllables are marked by hyphens and a prime mark ('), with the stressed syllable preceding the prime. Long vowels are pronounced as follows: ā (say), ē (keep), ī (high), ō (oat), ū (rule). G always indicates a hard sound (god) and j a soft one (giant).

Achilles	ākil′ ēz
Aegean	ājē′ an
aegis	ē′ jis
Aeschylus	es′ ki-lus
Aethiopis	ī thē′-ō-pis
Aidoneus	ī-dō′nē-us
or	ī-dō′ nūs
Aigai	ī′ gī
Alcman	alk′ man
Alkmene	alk-mē′ nē
Alpheios	al-fā′ os
ambrosia	am-brō′ zha
Amphitrite	am-fī trī′-tē
Amphitryon:	am-fi′ trē-on
Anacreon	an-ak′ rē-on
Anchises	an-kī′ sēz
Antoninus Liberalis	an-tō-nī′ nus
	līber-a′ lis
Aphrodite	af-rō-dī′ tē
Apollo	āpol′ lō
Apollodorus	āpol-lō dō′ rus
Apollonius Rhodius	āpol-lō′ nē-us
	rhō′ dē-us
Archilochus	ar-kil′ ōkus
Arkadia	ar-kā′ dē-a
Argeiphontes	ar-gā-īfon′ tez
Argos	ar′ gos
Artemis	ar′ tēmis
Ares	ār′ ēz
Asklepios	as-klē′ pē-os
Athens	ath′ enz
Athena	āthē′ na
Atlas	at′ las
Bacchylides	bākil′ īdēz
Baubo	bau′ bō
Boiotia	bē-ō′sha
Caria	ka′ rē-a
Callinus	kal-līn′ us
Chaos	kā′ os
Chimera	kī-mair′ a
Chios	kē′ os
Chrysaor	krisa′ ōr
or	krū-sa′ ōr
Crete	krēt

Cypria	si′ prē-a
Cyprus	sī′ prus
Dardanos	dar′ dan-os
Delos	dē′ los
Delphi	del′ fī
Delphinios	del-fi′ nē-os
Demeter	demē′ ter
Demo	de′ mō
Demophoön	demo′ fō-on
Deo	de′ ō
Diodorus Siculus	dī-ō-dor′ us
	si′ kulus
Diokles/Dioclos	dī′ oklēz
or	dī′ oklos
Dione	dī-ō′ nē
Dionysos	dī-ō-nī′ sos
Dioskouroi	dē-os-kū-roy
Dolichos	dol′ ikos
Echidna	ekid′ na
Eileithyia	ā-lā-thwē′ a
elegy	e′ lejē
Eleusis	el-ū′ sis
Endymion	en-di′ mē-on
Eos	ē′ os
Epigoni	ep-ig′ on-ē
Eratosthenes	er-atos′ thenēz
Erebos	e′ rebos
Eros	e′ ros
Euboia	ū-bē′ a
Eumolpos	ū-mol′ pos
Eurynome	urin′ ō-mē
Eurystheus	uris′ thē-us
or	uris′ thūs
Gaia	gī′ a
Ganymede	gan′ imēd
Hades	hā′ dēz
Harmonia	har-mō-nē′ a
Hebe	hē′ bē
Hekate	he′ katē
Helikon	he′ likon
Helios	hē′ lē-os
Hephaistos	hefīs′ tos
or	hefes′ tus

168

Hera	hair' a	Musaeus	mū-sā' us
Herakles	hair' aklēz	Nausikaä	now-sik' ā-a
Hermes	her' mēz	Naxos	naks' os
Hesiod	hē' sē-od	Nereus	nār' ē-us
Hestia	hes' tē-a	or	nār' ūs
Homer	hō' mur	Nysa	nī' sa
Horai	ho' rī	Odysseus	ō-di' sē-us
hubris	hū' bris	or	ō-di' sūs
Hyperboreans	hī-per-bōr-ē' anz	Odyssey	o' disē
Hyperion	hī-pēr' ē-on	Oedipodeia	ed-ē-podā' a
Iambe	ī-am' bē	Okeanos	ō-kā' anos
Ibykos	i' bikos	Olympos	ō-lim' pos
Ida	ī' da	Onchestos	on-kes' tos
Ilion	il' ē-on	Orpheus	ōr' fē-us
Iliad	il' ē-ad	Ortygia	ōr-tig' ē-a
Ionia	ī-ōn' ē-a	Ouranos	ū' ranos
Iris	ī' ris	paean	pī' an
Kadmos	kad' mos	or	pē' an
Kallidike	kal-li' di-kē	Pallas	pal' las
Kalliope	kal-lī'ō-pē	Pandora	pan-dōr' a
Kalypso	kalip' sō	Paphos	pa' fos
Kastor	kas' tōr	Parnassos	par-nas' sos
Keleos	kē' lē-os	Paros	par' os
kêrux	kā' rūks	Peloponnesos	pel-opon-nē' sos
kerykeion	ker-ū' kē-on	Pelops	pē' lops
Kirke	kir' kē	Persephone	per-sef' ō-nē
often pronounced sir' sē (= Circe)		Phoibos	fē' bos
Klaros	kla' ros	Phrygia	fri' jē-a
Knossos	kno' sos	Pieria	pē-air' ē-a
Koios	koy' os	Polydeukes	pol-i dū' kēz
Kore	kōr' ā	Polyxeinos	pol-ik' sā-nos
Koronis	korōn' is	Pontos	pon' tos
Krisa	kri' sa	Poseidon	pō-sī' don
Kronios	kro' nē-os	Priam	prī' am
Kronos	kro' nos	prooimion	prō-ē' mē-on
Kybele	ki' bilē	Pylos	pī' los
often pronounced si'belē (=Cybele)		Pytho	pī' thō
kykeion	kikē' on	Pythia	pi' thē-a
kylix	kī' liks	Rharion	ra' rē-on
Kyllene	kī-lē' nē	Rhea	rā' a
Kynthos	kin' thos	Samos	sā' mos
Kynthaios	kin-thī' os	Sappho	saf' fō
Kythera	kith' er-a	Selene	selē' nē
Kytherea	kith-er' ē-a	Semele	se' melē
Leda	lē' da	Semonides	semon' idēz
Lesbos	lez' bos	Silenoi	sī-lē' noy
Leto	lē' tō	Simonides	sī-mon' idēz
maenad	mē' nad	Stesichoros	stesik' or-os
Maia	mī' a	Styx	stiks
Makar	ma' kar	Syrinx	sir' inks
Mekone	mā' konē	Tartaros	tar' tar-os
Metaneira	metanā' ra	Taygetos	tī-ā' getos
Metis	mā' tis	Telegony	tele' gon-ē
Minos	mī' nos	Telphousa	tel-fū' sa
Mnemosyne	nemos' ū-nā	Tethys	te' this
or	nemos' ū-nē	Thebes	thēbz

Theia	thā' a
Themis, themis	the' mis
Theognis	thē-og' nis
Thesmophoria	thez-mofor' ē-a
Thessaly	thes' salē
Thetis	thē' tis
timê	timā'
Tithonos	tithō' nos
Titanomachy	tī-tan-o' mak-ē
Titans	tī' tanz
Triptolemos	trip-tol' emos
Tritogeneia	tri' togen-ā-a
Tros	trōs
Tyndareus	tin-dar' eus
Tyndaridai	tin-dar' idī
Typhaon	tī-fa' on
Typhoeus	tī-fē' us
Zeus	zūs

SUGGESTIONS FOR FURTHER READING

While the bibliography in English on the Homeric Hymns is not vast, an enormous amount has been written on Greek mythology and religion. What follows is a heartlessly brief selection of works to introduce the reader to various approaches to the study of the hymns and their myths. The bibliographies in many of these works will provide more extensive suggestions for further reading.

1. **Standard Commentaries on the Greek Text of the Hymns**

   Allen, T.W., and E.E. Sikes, eds. *The Homeric Hymns* (London 1904)

   Allen, T.W., W.R. Halliday, and E.E. Sikes, eds. *The Homeric Hymns* (Oxford 1936)

   Càssola, F., ed. *Inni Omerici* (Milan 1975) [in Italian]

2. **Works Related to the Major Hymns**

   Boedeker, D.D. Aphrodite's Entry Into Greek Epic, *Mnemosyne Supplement* 32 (Leiden 1974)

   Brown, N.O. *Hermes the Thief* (New York 1947)

   Clay, J.S. *The Politics of Olympus* (Princeton 1989)

   Foley, H.P. *The Homeric Hymn to Demeter* (Princeton 1994)

   Fontenrose, J. *Python: A Study of Delphic Myth and Its Origins* (Berkeley 1959)

   Janko, R. *Homer, Hesiod and the Hymns: Diachronic Development in Epic Diction* (Cambridge 1982)

   Miller, A. From Delos to Delphi: A Literary Study of the *Homeric Hymn to Apollo*, *Mnemosyne Supplement* 93 (Leiden 1986)

   Preziosi, P.G. "The *Homeric Hymn to Aphrodite*. An Oral Analysis," *Harvard Studies in Classical Philology* 71 (1966) 171-204

   Richardson, N.J. *The Homeric Hymn to Demeter* (Oxford 1974)

   Segal, C. "The *Homeric Hymn to Aphrodite*: A Structuralist Approach," *Classical World* 67 (1974) 205-212

   Shelmerdine, S.C. "Hermes and the Tortoise: A Prelude to Cult," *Greek, Roman and Byzantine Studies* 25 (1984) 201-207

   _____ "Odyssean Allusions in the Fourth Homeric Hymn," *Transactions and Proceedings of the American Philological Association* 116 (1986) 49-63

   Smith, P.M. Nursling of Immortality: A Study of the *Homeric Hymn to Aphrodite*. *Studien zur klassischen Philologie* 3 (Frankfurt 1981)

Sowa, C.A. *Traditional Themes and the Homeric Hymns* (Chicago 1984)

3. **General Works on Greek Mythology and Religion**

Apollodorus. *The Library*, 2 vols. with an English translation and notes by J.G. Frazer (London and Cambridge, MA 1921)

Bremmer, J. (ed.). *Interpretations of Greek Mythology* (London and Sydney 1987)

Burkert, W. *Greek Religion* (Stuttgart 1977; Eng. trans. Cambridge, MA 1985)

Carpenter, T. *Art and Myth in Ancient Greece* (London and New York 1991)

Easterling, P.E. and J.V. Muir (eds.). *Greek Religion and Society* (Cambridge 1985)

Edmonds, L. (ed.). *Approaches to Greek Myth* (Baltimore 1990)

Gordon, R.L. (ed.). *Myth, Religion and Society* (Cambridge 1981)

Kirk, G.S. *Myth: Its Meaning and Functions in Ancient and Other Cultures* (Berkeley and Los Angeles 1970)

Mayerson, P. *Classical Mythology in Literature, Art, and Music* (Waltham, MA 1971)

Morford, M.P.O. and R.J. Lenardon. *Classical Mythology* (New York and London 1991)

Nagy, G. *Greek Mythology and Poetics* (Ithaca and London 1990)

Parke, H.W. *Festivals of the Athenians* (Ithaca, N.Y. 1977)

Thalmann, W.G. *Conventions of Form and Thought in Early Greek Epic Poetry* (Baltimore 1984)

Vernant, P. *Myth and Thought Among the Greeks* (Paris 1975, 3rd. ed. 1985; Eng. trans. London 1983)

Zaidman, L.B. and P.S. Pantel. *Religion in the Ancient Greek City* (Paris 1989; Eng. trans. Cambridge 1992)

References to the text of the hymns are given in line numbers, with "n" to indicate footnotes; references to the introductions are given in page numbers. Most names are listed in their Greek form, with common Latin spellings or Latin names given in square brackets, followed by brief identifications.